The Joy of Investing

with Marco Turco

I0037024

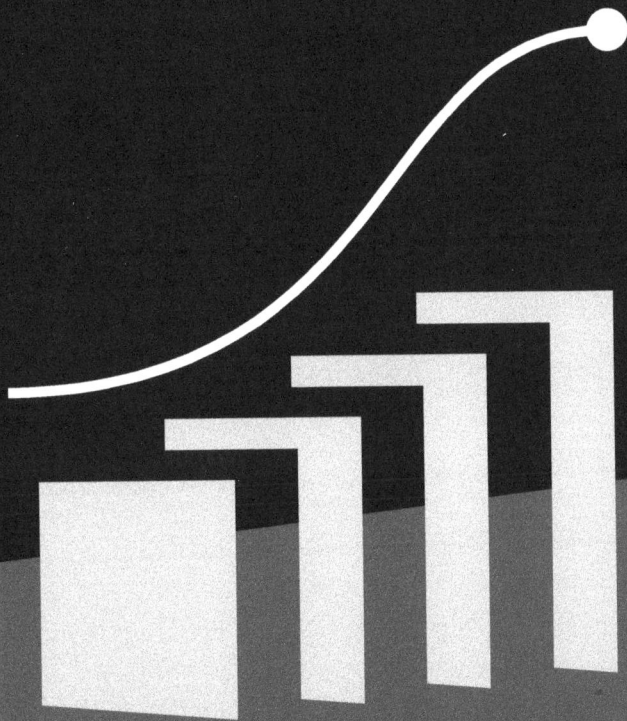

" Sometimes the Investor is so wrong he is right "

A sunrisewise publication

Index

FOREWORD BY THE AUTHOR

This handbook is a book, a guide and a workbook too. It is divided into three sections.

1.Temperament
2.Technical skills
3.Margin of safety

You will find paragraphs about "how to pick stocks". However, you will find a lot of concepts that are more about a philosophy of investing and temperament than mere technical skills. Without some temperamental qualities and the right attitude towards the market, technical skills of any kind can be ineffective. The "joy of investing" comes more from the former than the latter, and with it also the "outstanding results".
Being average in investing can come about for anyone. Being above average and getting rich is another story.
The right blueprint to getting rich comes into being first in your mind and your education.
While life (and your stocks portfolio) will have its ups and downs, consistently saving, continuingly learning, thinking for yourself, developing good habits, focusing on the long term and having fun along the way is what you need to set yourself up for success in life.
It's as simple as that. Remember: it's simple but not easy to achieve.

And if you also agree with me and Buffett that "Happiness is not about how much you spend", this book is definitely for you.

Following its principles and with "Value Investing" as a guide, you will probably end up having more money than needed to be happy. I hope to help you accumulate knowledge and pile up enough money so that a good portion of it won't be needed to bring any more happiness in your life. I hope you are generous and lovable because money will make you more of what you already are. You will not only be free and independent but I'm sure you will use the "more" you've piled up, to help others. That is the real Joy of Investing.

" WHAT IS VALUE INVESTING? "

Value Investing" is every intelligent investment based upon value. To lay out a sum of money today to get more in the future is a "Value decision" and a "Value equation". It's usually, but not always, a more profitable and safer decision to make, in comparison to other investing opportunities that are based on a calculation of a disparity between what you get and the price you pay for it. It certainly uses a margin of safety and an adequate body of notions based upon facts, and reasoning based upon experience. It is underpinned by rationality and a temperament that are able to completely disregard what the others think about its conclusion.

Note: Ben Graham never gave a precise definition of "Value Investing" nor ever used the expression. No surprise to me at all. By first defining "Investing" versus "Speculation" in "Security Analysis" and then going on to explain the concept of "The Intelligent Investor" was enough to recognize that every true form of "Investing" is "Value Investing".
The definition above came to me through years spent every day with Graham and Buffett. It is what I used and continue to use in making my stock picks and investment decisions.

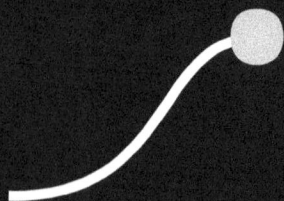

Section one:
Temperament

FOCUS

One of my favorite quotes of Warren Buffett (which I put on the back of one of my t-shirts) is: "A short focus is not conducive to long profits".

If you are not focused, if you are not determined, not almost obsessed by the will of achieving your goals and getting where you want, you are not going to make it. You won't become what you want to be. I know that it may be hard to hear but it's fair to say that a lot of people are frustrated at the end of their lives because they recognize they didn't focus enough. The truth of the matter is they didn't push hard enough when it was the right time. Since I was a kid, I've loved memorizing different extracts, such as a passage of Shakespeare or Dante. I probably did it to impress people, although some adults told me it wasn't a good idea or even useful. It turned out to be a wonderful exercise. When I started memorizing Buffett's quotes and all he said about investing, I realized how useful and powerful this ability could be. Some passages from "The intelligent investor" by Ben Graham, especially from chapter 8 and 20 (as suggested by Warren Buffett) saved my life at certain times because I was able to perfectly recall them. Buffett did the same too with the books that he loved as a young student.

ESTABLISH A SCHEDULE

It's a hard task to establish a schedule for your activities. Set aside 4-hours of study-time in the morning, then 3 hours in the afternoon and another hour or so before going to bed. It IS hard but doable, even if few do so. If you set your mind to undertaking this extra-work, if you are able find the strength and drive inside of yourself, if you are consistent, then you will be successful in whatever you desire. But you have to follow this program every day, Saturdays and Sundays included, and you have to have a plan.

If you do so and you have patience, sooner or later, your time will come. Your sacrifice and the hard work you put in will pay off.

BAD DAYS AND HABITS

We are all human and we have to deal with bad days every once in a while. On those days, my advice is to find the strength to keep on going and do your best to get to the end of the day, having accomplished at least something productive. No matter what. This will make a difference in reaching your goal and you'll eventually gain the upper hand over your peers. The commitment and hard work, the effort you put in, not just for a day or a week or a month, but consistently for years will be the reason why you end up rich and independent. It is beneficial to know this and put it into practice from a very young age. It is, in fact, so true that "the chain of habit is so light to be felt that soon become too heavy to be broken".

That is also the reason why good teachers and good models are so important. With the right mentors, it is much easier to develop the right habits from a young age. And this will make a difference; it really can change the outcome of your life. And if you are not a kid anymore, don't get discouraged. It's never too late to do the right thing.

EXTRA-EFFORT = EXTRA INCOME

In my course, I teach my students how to achieve the technical skills and knowledge they need to develop themselves. Almost everybody can learn that. I can teach you my own way of sifting through all the data currently available on which companies to invest in. We can study many case histories of the successful stocks I bought to build up useful experience and knowledge. It's certainly a necessary step to make money. But nothing is for granted and there's a price for every reward. This price can be hours of sweat, and maybe even tears. Don't trust any guru-type knowledge. Luck may be involved to some extent, but there are no secrets or short-cuts in the investment world. You can make it in this business without having an extremely high IQ. Buffett said that it's enough to have the IQ required for driving from here to "downtown Omaha". So, we are not on a mission to do something special to be special. But you must be persistent. You have to focus and have resolution and consistency. Discipline and the right emotional stability are a must. Anybody can get lucky and luck does play a part in everybody's life; however, as Seneca stated: "the special characteristic of a great person is to triumph over the disasters and panics of human life". In response to the question, "How did you do that?" or "How did you become rich?", the most beautiful and perfect answer is: "I was ready to deserve it. I was ready to make the extra-effort."

It's amazing how this effort is possible for everyone to do but few usually make it. You need to detach yourself from the crowd and focus on your dreams; on where you want to be 10 or 20 years from now. A mentor or a coach can usually help keep you on track because it is not easy to do it on your own, 8 hours a day, every day, come hell or high water.

Now, let's see how this can be practiced and achieved. A day is longer than 8 hours. Everybody knows that. But what everybody doesn't know it's how to prioritize things and say no to wasting time.

PRIORITIZE YOUR GOALS

If your goal is to make more money, accumulate wealth, and prepare for a more comfortable future or retirement, consider those 8 hours a day and make a plan. Find the right mentors, the right course, learn from ace investors. Focus on your goal, make a long-term plan, and then write down some check points along the way. Every three-five years, for example, see if you are heading in the right direction and what adjustments should be made. Then start working on correcting them week by week, one step at the time. Your plan may be demanding so don't be too tough on yourself about what you still have to accomplish. Conversely, be happy with what you have accomplished so far. Do appreciate what you have and the progress you have made. To earn more is not enough. You have to spend less (at least for the time being) to cumulate wealth. You have to adjust your cost-structure to your income to better educate yourself in managing money. If you are trying to adjust your income to the cost-structure, it's likely you are mismanaging your money. And the reason is simple: you are just starting to learn the "prolific nature of money". It's going to be a long journey, but the very first success will help open your mind and see how beneficial it can be to invest the retained earnings that were previously spent unnecessarily. Now you've finally started your plan. There will be twists and turns, some bumps along the road are unavoidable but this new plan will take you where you want to go. A coach/mentor will help you enormously in keeping track of your results; checking if you've got back on track and are on target with the plan. Remember that an "Idiot with a plan can beat a genius without a plan". Many people are undecided about what they really want to achieve in life. That's why they often change their goals or plans, they don't know where they want to go; hence, they go nowhere.

RELY UPON YOUR INTELLIGENCE

Don't complain. Don't criticize, don't blame others, don't come up with lame excuses to put things off. Don't look back. Use your brain and then act! Practice! Everyday. Don't take polls about where your life should be going. Use your reasoned choice to make thoughtful decisions. Use your brain and intelligence, the most precious asset you may have. Rely upon your intelligence. Use it to your advantage. Before any important financial decision, ask yourself: "What is the most rational thing to do?" Rationality will lead you to the best decision financially.

DON'T BE AFRAID

If you think intensely about achieving something, it is very likely you will convert it into action. And only good and positive thoughts will bring you good and positive things. You have the capability of erasing the pessimism, erasing the thoughts that bring you down. Don't be a downer to yourself. You will meet a lot of people that will try to put you down; say you are not going anywhere and you are a dreamer. Don't do that to yourself. Many will tell you that you can't be what you want to be in life. That it is just dreaming. Ask them if they've ever tried doing a job that they love or ever tried living their lives following their passion. You'll discover they've never tried, or they tried for a month or two and then they gave up. Great people and successful people will never belittle you. They will encourage you and also give you sound advice. They have been before where you are now.

Also don't be afraid to ask. If you want something, you have to stop being afraid to ask. Don't be bashful, don't be scared by getting "no" for an answer either. Just move forward. Don't be scared to speak out and let others know you want help.

HAVE A PLAN

Make a long, very long-term plan. Set goals for where you see yourself 10-20 years from now. Then set some intermediate steps to get there. Call them check points, they can be somewhere between every 3-5 years. Then proceed to do something, week after week and day after day. Every 3- 6 months, look back at what you accomplished. Check where you are and if you are headed toward your long-term goals. Be flexible and ready to make reasonable adjustments all the while sticking with the overall plan. Be patient. Be consistent. Don't get discouraged if sometimes you feel tired or as if you aren't going anywhere. It's good to take a break and rest. Take a walk or have a nice day-off. Recharge until you feel well and ready to re-start your engine. As I've said before, you have to embrace the sacrifice, you have to enjoy the journey. Start small, one step at the time, but remember it's not a sin to think big.

BE CONFIDENT

When he was a young boy, Warren Buffett said to his younger sister, Bertie, that he wanted to be a millionaire by the age of 30. And "millionaire" in the 40s was like saying "billionaire" in present times. He didn't say "I want to have my own small business" or "I want to have a grocery store like grandpa". I will say it again, it's not a sin to think big. It will guide and feed your thoughts, unleashing the best in you. Buffett set for himself a regimented frame of rules; a precise discipline that he never strays from. As his other sister Doris once said: "Warren never breaks a rule". Look at what he's accomplished. He's not only became a millionaire but became the chairman and soul of Berkshire Hathaway, a corporate extension of himself. Literally. The only holding company created basically from scratch, that a few years ago become the fourth biggest market capitalization on Wall Street, and is still in the top ten nowadays.

SWEAT EQUITY WORKS

A 'financial planner' friend of mine once used an expression I really like: "Sweat Equity". He was remembering his first years making phone calls to prospective clients trying to build up his own customer portfolio. Now he is successful and manages a sizeable portfolio of clients and their assets. A successful business provides a service that is in high demand and has as many clients as it can manage and serve well. Customer care means success. How much capital was required to build such a business? Almost zero. In 2006 I started my RE Brokerage company. It was all sweat equity. I started with no more than 300 euros of capital. My office was basically my car, a cell phone and a laptop of the time, no smart phones yet. After three months of hard work, I sold my first house; closing a very good deal for my clients and therefore providing myself with a very good commission. I realized I was sweating my equity. The first success always gives you the excitement to continue. I started to sell and rent for at least 12-15k gross income a month. Debt over equity = zero. All the retained earnings were ready to be invested in the stock market in the USA. Some monies I allocated to improve my image and to advertise. For years my office remained 'an office by the hour', until I bought an entire commercial facility. Unconsciously I loved the same businesses that Buffett loves: the ones that require few capital expenses. CAPEX must be low, because if you are not careful, it can someday transform all your sweat in tears.

ENJOY THE JOURNEY

If you think about being rich one day, chances are that you will be rich someday. The sooner you wake up and start the process, the sooner you will look around to see how you can learn from the best investors, the best business minds, the money-makers. If you start from there, you can see that your thoughts and determination can win. Find the right models. To overcome bad circumstances and win over adversities is like fighting on the court in the NBA. The right coach is essential. And you have to have faith. Belief is also trying the "impossible" sometimes. Set realistic goals and proceed one step at the time but don't set a limit. If you set a limit, you become your limit. You've decided to step out of the crowd and go where the adventure is. So, now it's time to hit the road.

"BUT I'M NO WARREN BUFFETT"

Good point. Sure! I have good news: you don't have to be. Nobody is. But there are a lot of people that did very well following the same path he followed. They found their own way. Each of us finds what is enough for ourselves, it is strictly subjective; enough is never too little when you achieve your goals and dreams.
I have three things for you to consider; I hope you will find them exhausting and interesting enough to make you start your journey in the magic world of investing.

1.HARD WORK CAN BE FUN

I agree that nobody is as smart as Warren Buffett when it comes to investing. So, let's work even harder! You may never become Caravaggio one day but nonetheless, the more you paint the better your next painting will be. The more you are ready to put in the necessary work, chances are that your best investment decision will be the next one you make. Read 600 pages a week instead of the 500 Warren does. I know im establishing a very high bar here. But there is a reason: I want you to consider how huge is the power of Passion and Education. They are like dynamite if combined together. Just make sure you have both. Make sure what you are trying to do is really your long-life dream. Then, everything is possible.

2.THE CAGE IS ONLY IN YOUR MIND, THEREFORE YOU CAN CONTROL IT

In the end, reaching a precise level of wealth or success to be happy isn't needed. As you aren't putting any ceiling or limit on yourself and what you can do, you aren't setting an exact figure or number for what is your minimum standard of "happiness". It simply doesn't work that way. Warren was just as happy with the 10,000 dollars saved after high school than later on when he had much more money. After a certain level of comfort in life (achievable with not that much money) the use you make of the surplus doesn't change your life that much. And the surplus of money you do not manage well can be easily lost. It can also affect your personal life; harming the relationships you have with family and friends, stealing away your happiness, all because you weren't well prepared to manage money or properly financially educated.

Financial illiteracy is a big problem all over the world. It really affects the lives of many people. Many people struggle with money problems, even if they have good paychecks. They are smart, decent and educated people in many areas, except in investing and managing their hard-earned income.

3.IT'S ALREADY HAPPENING

The key factor to understand is that you have to enjoy the journey, wherever it leads you. And it will lead you into a better position no matter what. The important fact is that you are interested in making a change. You've made a plan to improve your life and educate yourself. You will not only become a better person, but most likely a shrewd investor as well. So please make sure to love the process, love the adventure of trying something that most people are afraid to try. I will never get tired of stressing this important attitude. It's the building block that underpins all the rest of the project you are trying to develop*. **You have to love your own true colors and painting on your own canvas every day.***

LET'S START

Let's be practical. Start with paying off all of your credit card debt. Underspend your income, so that your first investment is not with borrowed money. Stop going to fancy restaurants or dining out very often. Ask yourself if what you are buying is really necessary or if such a large amount of it is necessary.

Anytime you overspend, you sell a piece of your future. It starts with understanding you can be happy by simply buying less and saving more; I know it's not going to happen overnight. If you are not saving anything from your income, I'm asking you to stop and make a change. Ask for help if you feel it is almost impossible, because you are wrong. You can save. No matter the amount saved, it is the "Joy of Investing".

IT'S NOT LUCK OR GAMBLING: IT WORKS

I also want to introduce you to some shrewd investors you can learn a lot from. In my course, I have some specific lessons dedicated to the lives, different strategies, and habits of the best value investors. They all became extremely successful and rich managing money. They loved making the extra-effort, like Buffett. Just like him, they jumped out of bed every morning to paint their canvas in the way they most wanted to. Ben Graham, Warren Buffett, Walter Schloss, Tom Knapp, Bill Ruane, Charlie Munger, Rick Guerin, Irving Khan. There are sets of lessons devoted to these greats and several others. In general, history and biographies of great people are the best books to read. You've probably already noticed that the greats of today read a lot about the lives of the greats of yesterday.

When it comes to "Value Investors", what do those great players have in common? They all had their own way of applying the same theory. They all used different colors on their palette and different choices of landscapes. They bought different stocks in the bull and bear markets. But their supreme technique, taught by Ben Graham, was the same. They were buying businesses for far below what they were worth. They tried to buy a dollar with 40 cents. No matter what Mr. Market and the crowd were going to do or were thinking about the present or the future. No matter the waiting time to accomplish the result, they were able to turn the odds in their favor when investing. They minimized the risk as much as they could using the "margin of safety" (so important that the entire third section of this book is about this safe net).

Their decisions were always "Value Decisions". They applied value judgment, all the time. They never forgot they wanted to acquire more than what they paid for. They used 'time' and the 'market' as their servants.
If this simple inoculation has had an immediate effect on you, it is time to dig into it more and take some steps together to make it work.

GOOD HABITS ARE LIKE A GYM

There are some techniques you can develop to become patient. There are some exercises you can do to act in spite of fear. There are ways to learn how to refrain from doing something. It is not easy and having a coach or somebody to help can be critical. Throughout the lessons in my course, I teach what worked for me. Temperament, I can never stress enough, is like the thumb of your hand. You can have the most brilliant qualities, tons of IQ, and knowledge but if your beautiful fingers are not strongly supported by your thumb, they will fall or fumble.

Buffett was born with the right temperament toward the market. I'm sure. But Buffett himself tells you that you can become the person you want to be, to an even higher degree than you can imagine.

There's one study of books that I cover in my course that brilliantly show how motivation wins over talent most of the time. The combination of the two can really move mountains, but the most relevant of the two is motivation. And a plan. Education combined with good habits works wonders.

If you really have the motivation and ambition to get better at something, you will train yourself with the appropriate frequency allows you to achieve your goal. I did it. You can do it too. If you are aware that an event can happen, like a market crash, you will prepare and react accordingly to your plan. You won't know when something is going to happen but you can anticipate what your emotional reaction will be. You can train yourself how to be in charge of your emotions and control them.

RATIONALITY BECOMES A HABIT

The amygdala is a part of your brain that you want to study and know as well as you can. It's the one that alerts you and drives you crazy when there's "panicking-situation" (like a fire alarm going off). It helps alert your senses and saves you from dangerous situations by making you run, for example. But it also activates itself when markets are down or in other different circumstances that seem to be dangerous, but really, they are not. And an amygdala hijack can make you do things you will regret for the rest of your life. That's why you have to be prepared to coyly shrug off all the noise and know what to do in those situations when everybody is panicking. In other words, you have to first calm down your amygdala and do what Napoleon once said: "The Genius is the one that does average in a dangerous situation when everybody around loses control". Work together with your pre-frontal cortex, the part of your brain that makes rational and long-term decisions. Rationality, like kindness and generosity, can become a habit, if you apply it continuously to your everyday life with intentionality and pleasure. You can attain the extra-ordinary ability of doing what you originally planned, regard-less of the circumstances. After doing it once, it will get easier to keep doing. Habits and experience work wonders. Habits are powerful. Rationality can become a habit. Give it a try.

A WORD FROM WARREN

The best piece of advice from Buffet on this was at a Nebraska Student meeting back in 2005. It confirms how motivation and habits can be mastered and be your successful
tools in investing and in life:

*"There's two things that can probably hold you back in getting the
full horse power out of your engine or whatever maybe. All of you
have big enough engines (...) (..but...)*

FIRST THING: EDUCATION

*"If you didn't have a chance to have a decent education in life it
wouldn't make any difference what that potential was because
you never un-lock it"*

That's why everything you can invest in courses, mentors,
or books to help you grow are worth the money invested. I
would add Ben Franklin's quote "If you think that education is
expensive, try ignorance". But let's get back to Buffett.

SECOND THING: HABITS

*"The second most important thing and equally as important, its
in terms of the habits that you develop, in terms of what you do
with yourself. When we hire people, we look for 3 qualities: we*

look for Integrity, we look for Intelligence, we look for Energy. But if they don't have the first one, Integrity, the other two will kill you. 'Cause if you hire someone without Integrity you really want him to be dumb and lazy, don't you? (...) Smart and energetic only goes with Integrity".

PRACTICAL ASPECTS WITH STOCKS

When you learn how to analyze a business, do your homework with resolution and attention. Focus. It may happen that the stock of a business will fall to the price you were looking for a year or two later. You may not have the chance to remember everything you studied. Write down and then file the essential ratios and figures of the business. Now you may want to listen to the news and find out why the price is falling. However, even when doing everything right, doubts and emotions will happen. Don't be swept away by them. It's time to buy at a discount. Trust your body of notion and competence. Many students tell me:" I knew that I was right, but stock was plunging and I didn't have the courage that I had before to act". You are more influenced by emotions than facts and reasoning in certain situations.

There are many ways to mitigate all this. Depending on the situation, you may want to learn how to buy in different ways, maybe in many or few blocks, to exploit as much as possible the price of the stock going down. If you can control your emotions and stay rational, you can really take advantage of the situation; calibrating your actions in a way that allows you to make a lot of money. Something you learned a few or even many years ago is now working in your favor. Don't miss the chance. Stay rational. As Buffett once said: "If it's raining gold, don't go out with a thimble."

KEEP SMILING

"It is more human to laugh at life than to lament it"
Seneca, On Tranquility of mind

What do you do with sadness? What is the advantage of being a victim and giving up? We all face obstacles that are outside our control. We gave our best effort, we acted to the best of our capabilities but nonetheless things went wrong. How will we react? Great people have great spirits. Great investors are prepared to face hurdles and adversities that happen regardless of their reasoned choice. The best reaction is to laugh at things rather than complain or blame someone else. What was Mr. Buffett's reaction when interviewed after Kraft Heinz went down significantly, writing off its good will, cutting the dividend and so on? I've always noticed that Buffett laughs when mentioning his "many mistakes". A long successful journey requires a large portion of mistakes. It's an 18-hole golf course. If you want to get to the clubhouse, you've got to play them all. The good and the bad. If you don't train yourself to keep up your spirits, anger or bad feelings will take control of your mind. Don't let them. Never. Never ever. Even when dealing with the result of a mistake or a poor decision, don't let anger dry up your reason. We all face bad decisions. Was it a good decision for Buffett to stay twenty years in the textile business when he bought Berkshire in 1965? Tranquility of mind and a lot of good subsequent acquisitions fixed a bad financial decision that he now remembers with a smile. If you can't laugh at things when they seem too hard, try at least to smile and move forward.

SURVIVORS NEVER VICTIMS

Generally speaking, there is a tendency to assume that a successful investor who is also a rich man, had everything going in his favor in life and business. If it is true that a degree of luck can't do any harm, it is also true that the real value and nature of a great business man and investor are revealed during the most difficult and challenging moments. Everybody can get lucky once in a lifetime but real success is based upon perseverance and resilience. Even during the worst economic and financial scenarios; in the face of trage-dies, the right temperament will always find the strength to endure. And survive.

STUDY INVESTORS AND BILLIONAIRES

Charlie Munger, VP of Berkshire Hathaway (now a famous billionaire), at the age of 30 suffered adversities that would make our everyday struggles seem like a walk in the park. He was in the middle of a painful divorce when his young son was diagnosed with cancer and hospitalized. In the fifties, health insurance was almost unheard of, therefore he faced almost crippling financial difficulties. During the day, in the hospital, he held the little hand of his dying son, and at night, cried alone on the sidewalk, struggling with what to do to save or help him. To make matters even worse, he also was struck down by an illness that caused him to almost completely lose sight in one of his eyes.

We can only imagine how strong he had to be of mind and body to survive such an ordeal. He fought back, never considering himself a victim. It wouldn't have helped him survive. He focused on overcoming a tragic situation. And he made it. He had to work first as a lawyer at a time when lawyers didn't make much. Then, he became a successful investor and made his first real money in real estate. After that, he met Warren Buffett (they are both from Omaha, Nebraska), became a portfolio manager, and formed a successful partnership with him. He also married again and today, at the age of 97, has 8 children, a long list of achievements in life and business, and many stories to tell.

What impression or emotional impact do the daily fluctuations and vagaries of the market have on a spirit like Charlie Munger's? How can Mr. Market possibly affect his temperamental qualities or diminish his rationality?

THE REVERSE TEST

Before outlining what investment is, using one of the teachings of Charlie Munger, let's say what investing is not. The capability of finding the opposite of what we are looking for is critical in the pursuit of the right temperament. And it's reverse thinking that can be very useful in the business and investing world. Actually, spotting things you don't want before discovering what you do want, is a marvelous technique to practice for every decision-making process in your life.

WHAT INVESTING IS NOT

In a "satirical" Italian movie (please forgive the author), a philosopher lectures about the beauty of enjoying "the now" and forgetting about doing something useful for future generations: "Why should we do something for them? In the end, what has posterity done for us?" he wonders.
Think about investing as the direct opposite of the previous quote. We must leave this world a much better place than how we found it. We owe previous generations for all the tremendous improvements we have now, in terms of medicine, technology, transportation and so forth. Savings and investments have done wonders for society. It is our duty to give back to society what we have been able to pile up. The rewards will be reaped not only by us, but also by our sonsand daughters, grandsons, and granddaughters.

WHAT INVESTING IS

Investing is betting with optimism for a better future, a better society, a better country.

Investing is buying a piece of the future, turning all our work (sweating and saving) into benefiting the entire society; contributing to the further progression of medicine and/or the production of goods and services.

If we are sitting in the shade today, it is because somebody planted a tree for us in the past. Benjamin Graham planted a tree for us in writing the "Intelligent Investor", and again with David Dodd "Security Analysis". Thanks to his efforts and clarity, his stupendous knowledge and achievements did not disappear; they are inspirational and profitable for all of us. There would be no Warren Buffett without Graham and no Berkshire without Buffett and Munger. And I wouldn't be here trying to share and pass along all the marvelous things I've learnt and experienced in life, thanks to them. The offspring of human ingenuity has such a huge present value it is almost impossible to measure.

In fact, what if the geniuses of the past and the present wouldn't have had at their disposal enough capital to start their projects and enterprises? There would be no Apple or Microsoft today.

MASTER YOUR DESIRE

I consider desire, not life, the opposite of death. Desire with a capital D. When somebody asks me "What make you jump out of bed in the morning?" My answer is "Desire". Life itself can be meaningless if you "sleepwalk through life". If you start your day with a sparkle, a burning, itching desire to do something good, you will achieve something and gain what you want. Start with the desire of learning; of living life to the fullest, of doing something meaningful for you and others. What makes a real difference is to keep going, in spite of bad days, bad luck or adversity. It will lead you somewhere good, someday. If you live your life constantly afraid of failing, you are not going to go very far. Temperament helps you master your "Desire" in such a way to get where you want to go.

If your desire, like mine, was that of being rich; to be free and independent, not be forced to work 9 to 5, the stock market is the place to be. It has always been and will always be. But you need to learn a lot about how it works and about your-self. You have to be able to master yourself and your desires. That's why section one is so important. Your desire will help you overcome your fear of the water. And that's excellent, if you only want to learn how to swim. But becoming a good or outstanding swimmer, requires much, much more.

TEST THE WATER

Buffett bought his first stock at 11 years old. Three shares of "City service preferred "at $38. After the stock went down, he felt it was a good idea to sell them after only 4 months, for 40 bucks, gaining a profit of $5.25. It was July of 1942. In the following 5 years, the stock grew to more than 200 dollars. For everyone, Buffett or not, the first step always tests the water.

YES, YOU CAN LOSE...

"The most worthless of mankind are not afraid to condemn in others the same disorders which they allow in themselves"
Edward Gibbon "The decline and fall of the Roman Empire"

Applaud others for the good qualities you'd like to have but are struggling to achieve. It is not only paramount to find the right mentors and models in life, it is also critical to spot immediately what doesn't work for you. If you think independently, chances are that most people will not agree with you. At other times though, you will find a lot of people supporting you in something that is clearly a mistake. To fail "conventionally" seems to be more acceptable than to fail "unconventionally". And in the investment world, to succeed unconventionally would be almost considered outrageous or at least an anomaly by many of those who didn't succeed at all. That's why most business schools considered Buffett and Munger (probably still do) a statistical anomaly. Outliers.

Warren would say that sometimes human nature has such a perverse tendency to complicate things that when applying too much of a simple thing like "rationality", it is considered an exception. Add to rationality a consistent curiosity and a lot of discipline and you will have the "outliers". I would add that for many of us, rationality's main enemy is: emotions. That's why our journey starts with learning how to train our emotional side for being joyful in the investment world, especially when it comes to investing in common stocks. It starts with tempe-rament. It starts with patience. Observe yourself and others. Recognize your strengths and weaknesses. Be ready to cri-ticize yourself and learn from others. One of the best pieces of advice I got from Buffett was to write down the qualities of your heroes and also all the traits of the people you really don't like. The ones that make your stomach churn. Write down who you really don't want to be. Then remind yourself that It's hard to change but it's doable. **Yes, you can lose, but only if you don't try.**

BOOKS AND INVESTING GUIDES

There are so many books out there about investing, trading, money (in general) and finance that it can be really overwhelming if you don't already have in mind what your investment philosophy is. Talent can be a pursued interest but you have to know what you are interested in.

But how to establish a philosophy if you are just starting your journey and don't really know what to read? How can you find your way?

One of the reasons I'm writing this little guide is because I know how difficult can be to find exactly what type of game you should play in the investment world. It can take many years of going down the wrong, albeit entertaining, path to figure it out. More so, it can also be detrimental to you if you play a game, like trading, and then discover it doesn't work with your personality.

You have to build up the skills that are efficient for playing your game. The game you like. The one your mind and personality are suited for. The "Value Investing" approach will help you in many fields of business and areas of economic activity. I strongly recommend that you dig into it as much as you can. If this sounds like something that intrigues you, you will definitely save a lot of time and money following it, and not trying to apply the arcane and subtle technique for investing and asset management that are out there. And I'm confident you will know right away if it is for you. As Buffett wrote in

"The Super Investors of Graham and Doddsville" it is like an inoculation. If it gets you, it does it immediately. If it doesn't and you don't feel that the search for "Value" is the only true investment method (one that can be repeated and successfully practiced over and over again), than it's simply not going to work. No matter how much data or however many facts, stories and graphs are presented to you. All the wonderful investments you can make have to be built on the premise that is never overly repeated: every intelligent investment is based upon "Value". A "Value" decision and a "Value" equation if you like. You are looking for a much more long-term, profitable, and safer opportunity than in other investing operations; one that uses a margin of safety and an adequate body of notions based upon facts and experience. It all starts with the right attitude. Once you get it, you can further develop this attitude, which gets better and better as time goes by. You will accumulate more and more knowledge and profit over time. You don't need a high IQ to put all this into practice, but you will need to have a proper emotional foundation. Part of it is already inside you. You just have to find a guide to help you unleash your potential.

TO GUIDE YOU AND SAVE TIME

To do so, we will look for the right books and articles to guide you and not mislead you along the journey. The list of publications through the decades about "Value Investing" is pretty long. But in my opinion, the essential books to read are few. The most important thing is to read them very carefully and multiple times. It took me almost twenty years to narrow down the list of good books. There are roughly 2000 books about "Value Investing" and Buffett, but really only a few are worth reading and can help shape your investment philosophy and actions. Videos from the shareholders meeting are crucial. And of course, every one of Buffett's letters to shareholders (starting with the first partnerships in the fifties) is a gold mine and is really worth reading multiple times.

The main purpose of my course is to guide you and save you time (in fact years), in selecting the right materials out the ocean of information available. Over the last twenty years, I've done the homework for you, so to speak. Some things can immediately be utilized, others will take time to understand. Be that as it may, it truly was a lot work and took me much time and effort to sift through the gold mine of substance to find the real gems. The ones that succeeded in helping me acquire the wisdom and knowledge on how to invest.

There are also some other books I will suggest you read during my course that are not specifically about "Value Investing" but are good books just the same. There is a huge variety of knowledge and interests that can be useful to a professional investor or good investor. And unpredictable. You can find something useful and inspirational about many subjects. And it might work for you but not for others. Combined with the wisdom of investors like Graham and Buffett, it can make you rich. You will see opportunities where I haven't. That's why the "joy" and the "voyage" quickly become pretty personal. You just have to implement the right amount of interest, passion and work. And that's in your control. You can do it. So let's bring in the brushes, a palette with nice colors, and let's start to paint this canvas.

DIVERSIFICATION

Philip Fisher used to only own few stocks, averaging 5-6 in his portfolio. He used to keep them for a very, very long time. Warren Buffett owns just one stock. Since 1965. Berkshire Hathaway. Walter Schloss used to own 100. Why is there such a difference in how they do things if they come from the same intellectual framework, admire each other as investors and have almost the same investment philosophy and background?
Diversification can be such a controversial and debatable topic that it deserves at least a paragraph.

RISK

"Risk comes from not knowing what you are doing"
"Diversification is protection against ignorance"
Warren Buffett

Buffett's lines are always clear, simple and effective. They entice you to think and inspire you to know more.
Compare them with the following:

"Focus on proper risk management" = *"The three forms of diversification cover each factor of the return equation: the appropriate exposure beta to risk factors F, idiosyncratic risks (Greek letter) (...)" (SIC! "Note from the author")*
Hugues Langlois and Jacque Lussier
in "Rational Investing"
The subtleties of Asset Allocation
Columbia business School publishing

When you find something that is so well-researched and grounded in academic literature, be careful. It can kill you. Three forms of diversifications and exposures linked to factors like multiple Greek letters are of no use to you. I've read books such as the "Rational Investing", and studied the entire CFA course and preparation material, thousands of pages, to understand what to stay away from.
Diversification is one of those stereotypes in the investment world that professors of business schools find very easy to teach. Once you elect yourself as 'high priest' in the 'church of diversification', you can easily unleash your fantasy of creating many theories, systems, and equations. If you add some Greek letters to embellish the theory, making it more credible and complex, even better.

In the real world, if you are a no-nothing investor, you will need diversification. It will be your protection against ignorance. At some point, you no longer need to learn any theory: just expand the concept to its best version and buy an index fund. The S&P 500 is your best bet because you can diversify a lot of investing in all the major companies listed on Wall Street. You just bet on the future of corporate America as a whole, in the long-term, you will do fine. You don't know when to buy and what to buy. So, the solution is to continuously buy a little piece at the time. At certain times, you will buy high, other times you will do better buying at a lower price, but in the end, you will be ok. Not a bad thing for a no-nothing guy. You don't have to study, read, or worry about anything. Just be consistent....for your whole life.

If you feel you want to know more, (since you are reading this book, you must..), you will eventually learn how to pick the exactly right stocks for yourself. Only when you realize that the time to learn is now will you be eligible to find your own approach to diversification. Be careful. You will face many different options and strategies, but achieving an above average or outstanding result will be more like playing a 'hide–and-seek game' with yourself. Your investment philosophy about diversification must fit you and your personality. The subject, as I warned you, is deeply scrutinized by a lot of academicians. You will hear a lot of things and stereotypes. Again, think for yourself. If you study enough, your temperament and body of knowledge (underpinned by common sense and rationality), will bring you the joy of investing. The joy that comes from the freedom of making your own choices and conclusions.

I find the statement "Diversification is the only free meal in investing" and the 'Modern Portfolio Theory' to be "twaddle", just as Charlie Munger once said. Based upon my experience, I couldn't agree more. Therefore, I took some time in the next little paragraph to elaborate on it, but I really suggest: don't waste your time on theories, formula plans, pre-ordered systems, equations, different types of diversifications, Greek letters and so on so forth. They simply don't work and they never did in making money. They only work in teaching something for a considerable length of time to justify a paycheck.

A WOMAN ON A CART

As we said, if something is well-researched and grounded in academic literature, it seems to be the perfect lesson to teach. It will impress most people, especially other academicians. Unfortunately, it will not help you in any way learn the essence of business or the essence of investing in a business. There is certainly less glamour in studying a tiny immigrant woman from Russia who built from scratch the largest furniture shop in America. But it will certainly give you more than an idea of understanding what a good business is about and how it should be run. Mrs B of Nebraska Furniture was not able to read or write. She learnt English from her daughters when they came back home from elementary school. She knew what she was doing and had the humility to not venture into areas she didn't know. She had the determination to just humbly work hard on the one thing she was good at. She had the temperament and skills to run her own business and to be able to judge which people were right to have around her. She committed to putting all her energy into just one area until it was successful. And it took her many years. 16 years just to save enough to start her little business venture without any debt. And she stayed far enough away from debt as to be able to grow the business continuously, consistently, and with absolutely no-complacency, ever. She never changed or diversified her business model or mind. She started by selling cheaply and serving the customer; she did that her entire life with pleasure and tremendous success.

If you own a business like that, successful and well-managed, what kind of diversification do you need? You just need to make sure that it stays so and doesn't change. If you were to own a piece of Coca-Cola or some other wonderful, almost bullet-proof, business, wouldn't you just wish to have more of the same? Diversification is paramountly a "free lunch" or whatever they may call it, only for academicians but not for a business man. Diversification is not what a business man thinks about when he wakes up in the morning and uses his mind, energy, and rationality to get rich.

If an entrepreneur owns two or three of the best businesses in his hometown, you could say that he is very well diversified.

Now, what we don't understand is why in the stock market having less than 20-30 positions, many experts and professionals consider a portfolio not well-diversified? Furthermore, the risk calculation will also kick in, while the intricacies of the academic language and theories will do the rest to make simple concepts very complex. Stay away from that. Stay simple and consistent like Mrs B.

RISK OR VOLATILITY?

Volatility is opportunity. How can it be different? We love volatility. That's when you act by basing your action upon sound judgement. The business whose fundamentals you like goes down for some reason not related with its good economics. It's good news. Risk is not volatility. All things equal the price going down, which means putting the issue in a safer place, and your money too. The pundits from the above paragraph forgot about defining risk in an appropriate business-like way, and so decided to call it "volatility". It almost seems like they wanted your amygdala to go crazy when the stock is going down. If you don't know what you are doing, do a dumb thing: sell. If you do know what you are doing, you either don't do anything or if you are a true investor and saved some cash in preparation, do the right thing: buy more. We will talk about systemic risk some in my course, but above all, we will talk and study the most important risk to face: business risk. If you can develop experience and a base of sound knowledge concerning the risks of a business you understand, you will be able to disregard all the temporary risk associated with the macroeconomy; the price of oil, gold, cocoa beans or whatever the cable news throws at you on any given day. You want to carefully and keenly calculate the risks and measure the qualities of the business you looking to buy into. Its competitive advantage, its margins, its numbers in the past and what it shows currently in its financial reports. Accounting once again will help you face the risk. Risk can talk to you through the figures of the business. We will talk about it as much as possible during my one-to one- course on accounting. Being a Certified Financial Accountant isn't necessary, but accounting is the language of business. For that reason, it must become to some extent, our second language, in the wonderful country of common stocks and investing.

ACCOUNTING

Accounting is the language of business. When you buy a stock, you become a business owner and need to understand what goes on in your business. Financial reports tell you a story. It's a story that may seem very complicated at first, but you'll soon find it can be rather straightforward. I will teach you how to simplify the entire structures of:

An Income Statement
A Balance Sheet
A Cash Flow Statement

We will also go through the "sifting process" that is critical to saving time before the time comes to face your first 10k or 10Q. Many instruments are available on the internet that show the basic data of a public company, but not all of them are precise or reliable. I will be your guide through a 'redwood forest' of websites and sources that are sometimes very complex and difficult to understand. It may also be hard to figure out the correct "ratios" to select from all the thousands of companies out there. Ratios like "Debt over equity" for example, are a key component to the "sifting process" because they allow us to immediately disregard and eliminate companies that don't meet the test of what we are looking for in the 'Value Investment' universe.

Numbers and figures are there to paint a picture for the 'Intelligent Investor' that isn't hard to define or understand. If it's not understandable using your own reasoning or if it's not in your area of competence, you don't need to make a decision. Even if it's in your area of expertise and you have all the facts and numbers but they just don't lead you to a conclusion, you can move forward. It is a valuable lesson anyway. How to reach to a better conclusion will simply take time practicing and studying what worked well for me and many other investors in the past. During my course, we will study their approaches and different techniques. There is nothing more valuable than other's past experience to help you learn how to "feel your way" through the decision process of evalua-

ting a business. It's not difficult to tell when you don't like a company enough to buy it. It's more difficult to dig through a company's numbers and figure out what they are telling you about the business. And sometimes a boring company with a boring name, even with all its downsides, could be the one to invest in. It's another reward that comes with the 'joy of investing'. You will feel you are onto something. It can be a thrill, after going through many names and tickers of businesses that have been put on standby or discarded, to feel that the one you are analyzing could be the "one". But don't get overly excited, stay rational. And above all, learn to diligently follow through to the final step before you
open your wallet.

WRITE DOWN WHY

At this point, you have in your mind to buy this stock. It's how it goes. If you are following my course, you've learnt from me how to calculate the "earning power" and from your calculation, the price seems to be reasonable, if not attractive. You understand and like the business. You imagine how it will be 10 years from now and have the intention of keeping it for at least 5 years or forever. It depends on your reasoning and your personality. Of course, it additionally depends on how the future treats this business and how you assess it when and if changes do occur. But for now, we will establish together some "check points", such as the final question many investors ask themselves before buying anything (this will be covered in more detail during my course). The question I recommend you ask and I ask myself before buying is this: "Why am I spending hard-earned money on this?" Make sure you can come up with an answer that is at least two or three lines long. Start your answer with: "I'm buying Coca Cola because...". It's a simple but effective last step. It's a step that must be all yours and only yours. All that came before can be learnt from outside sources. But now, using reasoning based on facts, your personal history and your whole body of knowledge, the decision has to be all yours. This last step is something nobody can or should help you with.

A CASE HISTORY

After the first few lessons of my course, I describe the analysis of the reports and numbers of companies I've bought into. I further explain the reasoning that I used to conclude that they were in fact undervalued and safe enough to buy. Just one case will be briefly recounted and shown as an example out of many. The simplicity of the reasoning remains unchanged in the course and in my real life as an investor. If it's too complicated, it is not worth my effort or time spent studying. It means it is not a stock for me. In the investing business, we look for easy hurdles to jump. We don't want to train ourselves to jump very high hurdles that have more chances of failing.

MACERICH

On Sept 29th 2020, I was looking for some undervalued stock, and I just threw out a name (the abbreviation of a person I've known for a very long time) to see if there was a matching ticker. Yes, you got it right. I've profited more than once from a company I randomly found by throwing letters around. If it meets the requirements, I'll analyze the numbers of a business from a desert island. And this one did: MAC is the ticker of Macerich, a Real Estate Investment Trust. I started to scrutinize the numbers since this type of business is inside my area of competence. After my initial step of sifting through some basic ratios and numbers (how to do so will be explained in my course), I focused on what I'm most familiar with in this type of business: their collection of mall rentals. The second quarter of 2020 was a grim quarter for Macerich, the worst quarter ever, actually. I saw an opportunity linked to the pandemic (like many other opportunities present at the end of March 2020 and lasted for some months after). Prices of good businesses finally went down, making them good stocks to buy. The rental collection of MAC went down dramatically in 2020 but there were already some signs of recovery in September, and the occupancy rate only went slight down in 2017 until the present. The 1st and 2nd Quarter of 2020 occupancy rate was down to 91%, compared to 93% in 2019. A 2% difference is enough to scare Mr. Market, if he ever cared, but 2% is not significant to the intelligent investor, especially when there's other data that show advantages. But what data?

The first thing I always consider is debt. Short or long-term, I don't care. Debt goes against my nature and spirit. I know there is good debt and bad debt. But if I can avoid it, I do. Sometimes I miss out on some good financing opportunities, just to stay out of debt. It is just a part of my personality. It's a habit, a "forma mentis" (a "shape of the mind") that I discovered when I become party to the investment philosophy of investors like Schloss or Irving Khan. I was born in the south of Italy where good people stay away from debt, and even a mortgage on your house when I was a small kid was considered a bad financial habit. Money costs money was the lesson I learnt so you better try to earn and use your own. Back to Macerich, I kept on searching and found a note in my little book (where I file the stocks I analyze) that Macerich has 5 mortgages leveraged at less than 40% over equity and the company officially explained that "no significance change is expected". 1.5 billion of debt with a bank can be troublesome because it was set to expire in July 2021 but they were confident that would be re-financed. The main question was: "Could they

recover the back-rent in the future?" The pandemic wasn't hitting as hard anymore and 2 NY properties just re-opened. Furthermore, another 6 Californian properties re-opened and they were quite profitable before 2020. I didn't see any reason why in the future people wouldn't go back to shopping and malls would be up and running again like the good old times. It may take some time, depending on how long the pandemic lasts, but it will happen and shouldn't take that long.

What I noted in my little book was: "Retailers of MAC are recovering; the tenants are doing better but MAC as a company is not". That could be a lag to exploit, since the price of the stock was still depressed. Then I checked who were the 'Top Tenants' by rent in 2019: I put a + (plus) sign next to GAP, Victoria's secret, Footlocker, Banana Republic and a -(minus) sign minus next to Express and Macys. Also, I saw that JC Penney was in big trouble, but there were just two JC Penneys in Macerich's malls, and they could be replaced with new tenants.

I said to myself at this point: I have the facts, I have the numbers. I write down on a piece of paper my own evaluation of the business.

During every step of the process and with every number of my assessment, I use the margin of safety. If I have a prudent "9", I write down "8", and so on so forth. I come to a figure that is a very prudent, intrinsic value of roughly 1 billion. For the entire company. I don't need to impress anyone by writing a report in which I put a precise number like "1 ,089, 566, 459.19", with a cent to dollar ratio. It doesn't make sense. What makes sense it's that ideally, I feel even safer buying the whole MAC for 9 hundred million dollars. Another 10% discount on my groceries. That's the approach. Also you don't have to be too demanding all the time expecting to have "all" the data. It simply is not going to happen. Now, what if Mr. Market doesn't allow for any other discounts? I'll go with roughly 1 billion (that means about 7 dollars a share). At the time of my analysis, MAC was trading for $8 a share. A few days later, it went down to the price of $7 and a day after that, continued trading for $7. So, I placed a limit order for a moderately large block at $6.88. Before the end of the trading day, MAC went down and the order went through, in its entirety. I felt the joy of investing. I bought a piece of a business at the price I wanted to. I usually start with testing the water. This time, I made the largest bet I planned without waiting, but if MAC goes down any further, I always make sure I have some other ammunition to keep on buying.

LET'S FACE THE TRUTH

I didn't use any formula. No scientific calculator, no NPV, or FV or anything of the sort. I could if I wanted to and sometimes, I do, but most of the time, I run numbers in such a way that no scientific calculator is needed. I just use a regular one or a cell phone, or simply run the numbers in my mind. You know when you see a lady or a man you like. You know and in even shorter amount of time if you see something you don't like. In that case, I move forward immediately. I use a pen and write it all down in a little book (the one I'm using to help myself re-count all this to you). Yes, I file things in notebooks, or books

or agendas. I was born in 1976. I know myself; numbers stay in my mind this way, but not by typing them in on a laptop using excel or some other spreadsheets. It works perfectly well for me and I'm not going to change it. If you write what is really important to you on a piece of paper, it will be easier to remember and it will stick with you for a long time or forever. I've made money this way and I don't care what 7 billion people think about it. MAC went up to more than 14 dollars a share in less than one year (that is nothing, a blink of an eye for a true investor). So I made the happy mistake of selling the entire position. I wasn't expecting to double my money so fast. Now in December of 2021, I estimate the stock is around 20 dollar a share. I'm no Warren Buffett and I make a lot of mistakes, but like "Big Walt" Schloss I'm happy with that. I didn't lose. I successfully stayed away from what I don't like. And I do this constantly, with consistency and resolution. That's real investing. I make
money, I move forward. What I care about now is taking that money and doing it again. I know it's the hard part, so I don't look back. I focus. Again.

ALL KIND OF INFORMATIONS, ALL KINDS OF NOISE?

Before buying MAC at $6.88, I stumbled on other information about the company. In my little book, I had made a note that on Sept 29th, when MAC was trading with a Market Cap of 1.2B, an investor (I didn't know or had heard of before) named Ben Ashkewazy bought 75 million dollars of shares of MAC for his investment trust, at around 7 dollars a share. Days later during a conference call regarding the future of the company, it was stated that "It certainly isn't the right time to raise equity, trading at $8 a share today". Now bear in mind that I while don't completely disregard such rumors, they don't usually affect my decision about a business that's based upon facts and reasoning. Analysts reports, opinions, or an indication to buy/sell/hold or whatever, have no influence whatsoever on the process I've briefly described above. More so now than in Graham's time, I have to form an opinion about a company, because the companies trading below cash or book value (considering dependable assets) are almost all gone. There's none. But with the proper adjustments, you can still find "Value", further confirming Graham's principle. In a nutshell, you start with a "statistical approach" like him, but then you have to look at the business with a modern perspective. Your analysis should be modernized, following the same blueprint. You may not be as good as Warren Buffett, but it is doable. Consistency is the most difficult challenge. Anybody can be a good portfolio manager for a short period of time. Sounds results over a long period, that's a whole different story. Schloss kept on delivering breathtaking returns with his son for decades, until about 2005 when he decided to quit and retire. Buffett and Munger never quit learning but the framework is still the same. I too look at the business in a way that is less statistical than Graham's. It suits me very well because I don't have a bright, mathematical mind like he did. The fact that I was born in September of 1976, same year and month that he died, certainly plays in my favor in tackling the new challenge of applying his principles and teachings in a world that has changed so dramatically in the last two decades.

NPV, FV : THE VALUE IS NOT IN THE FORMULA

The "Value" is in the business, in its health and strengths. It's not in the formula you use. Because there's no formula. It's as simple as that. The "secret" is that there's no secret. The best investment made by the best investors were based on public information. Everybody had the same numbers and facts about The Washington Post in 1973, but only Buffett and Munger bought in few blocks 10% of the company. The "deal of a lifetime" exists and may happen. And if you live long enough, it may happen to you more than once, but you have to train yourself to be prepared. To calculate a "Net Present Value", a future "Value", and discounted stream of cash flow at the appropriate rate may require some formulas that are useful to know. They are easy too. We will learn how to intelligently use them. But remember: only if you train and prepare will the "real good deal" appear.

BEING WARPED AND A CONTRARIAN

Peter Lynch says in his book that if you pick 6 good stock out 10, you are a genius. I have 11 stocks in my portfolio and I'm doing well or even great with 10 of them. Am I a genius? I don't think so. But I'm confident of this: what I do and how I do it makes the difference. Because I'm really warped. I don't do what most people do. That's for sure. I don't even watch TV for very long periods of time. I read newspapers and just watch the news at night on my smart phone. I read all kinds of newspaper for free at the public library, where I also have access to a whole bunch of books and biographies. Many I end up buying because they're new and not available at the library.

I'm proud I don't feel the need to receive updates every waking moment. It suits me very well and I don't need to, I don't have to, and I don't want to take instant action in the market. I don't need to make decisions instantaneously. It's not the game I'm good at. As I see it, a real rich man is never in a hurry. If he's in a hurry, he is probably headed back towards poverty. And like I've said before, I hate losing money; I know from experience that poverty sucks. I enjoy the process of going at my own pace and I've learned that most of my personality traits are good for investing. However, I can always improve myself.

Sir John Templeton used to read the newspaper from the previous day when he was running his fund from the Bahamas in the 80s. In the years he spent there, he obtained better results in investing than in those of the years he'd spent on Wall Street. (And he was probably better off tax-wise, but that's my own assumption). I'll say it again: it's extremely unlikely that you will obtain good or outstanding results in the long term in investing, if you do what everybody else is doing or are content simply doing what the crowd is doing. True investing is not a fashion, it's a "style". "Style" is timeless. Fashion will perish and change sooner or later, "style" won't.

I like people and I love spending time with friends and family but some days are entirely spent reading and studying. From early in the morning to late night. It must be understood that sometimes this is critical for investing. I read a lot and every intelligent investor reads a lot. In order to properly take advantage of this privilege and not to lose it, results come if you are able to withdrawn yourself from everything for a bit. Some solitude is not only necessary, but beneficial. The biggest difference between Graham's time and now is that you have a lot more access to all kinds of financial and economic data. It's simply overwhelming. Because of this, undervalued assets are harder to find. But at the same time, we have more tools to access more markets and more companies than in the past. Opportunities are still numerous. But you have to have the right skills, discipline and patience. Combined together, you will at least do ok or well. With a little bit more effort, time and consistency (also a bit of luck), you can also do much more than just 'ok'. Only the stock market can give you this opportunity. And remember, luck happens when "a good opportunity meets a prepared mind"

MISTAKES

Enzo Ferrari used to put inside a cabinet the pieces of cars that didn't work well and caused an engine to fail or break down. He was fanatical about building engines that had to be powerful, light, and unique. They also had to sound good and be beautiful. What went wrong in this pursuit was just as important as what went right. So, learn from your mistakes and learn from the mistakes of others (which is even better to do). Find books, articles, videos about big and small financial disasters. Study them. Learn also from the small disasters or business mistakes of the people around you. You'll find out that complacency in some managers is often the reason why some wonderful business decline. You'll also find how greediness can lead to making poor decisions and in some cases, to a miserable life as well. Surprisingly enough, greed can obscure the sound judgements of very smart people.

I also want to remind you again what Buffett taught us about the two other factors that can hold you back, preventing you from unleashing your potential. They are: lack of education and bad habits. Tell yourself and your children everyday to stay away from them.

DON'T STRAY FROM YOUR AREA OF COMPETENCE

What can be dumber than to limit your potential in the area you care about most?

Define your area of competences. Play inside that area and don't venture outside it. If you don't know enough about a business, don't even consider investing money in it. If you feel you don't understand what is being proposed to you, don't you even try to figure out how you could make money with it. Buffett would say that "You don't have to win in every game". Even if it's fashionable and it has the kind of flair that appeals to you, you can't make money in a field that you don't have enough competence or education in. It's hard to learn and be expert in more than one area. Start with one.

DON'T TRUST PEOPLE YOU DON'T'LIKE

Don't prejudge anyone. That's important! But don't associate with people you don't like when it comes money. If they think far differently than you, if they behave in a way that makes your stomach churn, don't stick with them or the business proposition just because of a possible profit. It's not going to end well. It's one thing to have a customer with a bad attitude but a whole other thing to do business with a partner you are not in tune with and you don't like to be around. Good business associations are like a marriage. If you marry someone for just one reason, money, beauty or something else, as soon you lose interest in that area, you will lose interest in the business.

A WORD OF CAUTION

It's more likely you are going to make mistakes and misallocate capital when things are going well for yourself. You have extra cash, you feel smart and successful and you feel you are ready to make more money. As you may know, many emotions push you in a direction you probably wouldn't normally go. Again, temperament (discussed in section one) is key. Calm down, don't get overly excited, use your reasoned choice and rationality. Be in charge of your impulses. Don't be afraid of sitting on some cash if you don't see any good opportunity presenting itself. There is nothing wrong with that. It's wrong to lose money instead of just patiently waiting and saving for the right time.

FROM "CIGAR BUTTS" TO APPLE

Some say we climb over the shoulders of the giants of the past, trying to do our part in making a better world, a better future. All of your hours of focus, study and commitment will make sense for you and be beneficial to your community and society if you care about passing along what you've learnt. We can do our little part if we study the work of the greats of the past. It's like planting a tree today for others to sit under tomorrow. As Buffett wrote in his preface in the 4th edition of the "Intelligent Investor", Ben Graham planted the most important and robust tree for us under which we can now sit, implementing and modernizing some of concepts he gave us. That's what Buffett has done through the years. He will remain in history for showing us that timeless principles can be adapted to the most disruptive changes in technology, society or whatever. Buffett owes his tremendous success to his capability of adapting to modern products and businesses, using Graham's framework. We'll see in a moment how he updated his view of "Book Value" and "Value VS Growth". Probably the most important change he made was to his investment philosophy based on "Value", switching from "cheap stocks" and "bargains" (more available at smaller sums, the famous "Cigar Butts") to very wonderful businesses (he bought with much more capital at higher prices but looked for completely different basic characteristics).

A CHOICE OF TRUST

Becoming hugely successful and famous, Warren Buffett pushed forward this legacy, and added many new lessons. He has a long story of investment and business acquisitions from which we can learn and profit. He expanded the field of possibilities, showing how powerful the "Value Investing Philosophy" is and how timeless its method of acquiring growth is. I would be happy if you start today the life-long adventure of searching for value in your business and in your life. And the purpose of this book is to help you do that.

You'll find happiness and fulfillment; a new, free and independent vision of the world and the things around you. To focus on the value of things in comparison to their cost will be worth much more than just a business lesson. You will learn and gain more rewards than just knowing how to improve your allocation of money.

Now more than ever, during one of the largest bull market periods of all time, searching for "value" with Ben Graham and Buffett as guides, will serve you well. They will guarantee that tomorrow you gain the rewards you deserve to have today. Now that you have made your choice, you've stopped day-trading and are not obsessed anymore with looking at the prices of stocks every day or every hour. Let's see what we can do to alter the many stereotypes you've heard about the marketplace.

THE INVESTOR: WHO SHE OR HE IS

Every "investor" worthy to be called so is a "Value Investor" by nature. And every good "investment" worthy of being called so is a good "value decision" and so is a "Value Investment" by definition.

All other individuals or entities are speculators, not investors, and their operations are speculations not investments. Now, why is such an extreme, sharp distinction needed?

We are looking for the "joy of investing" because what we are looking for is a "joy" that will last. As long as possible. You may find the joy of speculating every now and then. There is nothing wrong with that,

just as there is nothing wrong with a nice, quick profit.

But you'll always have the dilemma while speculating of the "post-fugitive gain": how to reinvest the money in a short period of time. Dancing in and out from one speculation to another will simply enhance your chances of failing. The true Investor is ready to wait years to ripen the fruits of his pondered choice. Moreover, if he found a wonderful business to invest in, he is ready to own a piece of that business for decades. He sought for ages a business with the right characteristics and finally decided to participate in that business as an owner. He wants to cling to its stocks because he worked hard to figure out that it can be one of the most important decisions in his entire life. It is a permanent holding that can really compound money and give you a once in a life result you may never achieve otherwise. If it suits your portfolio, you can add more shares if the price goes down to a level you gauge as acceptable. Buffett started buying Berkshire at $7.00 a share in the sixties and he never sold any. As Charlie Munger once said, to find a wonderful business and "To stick with its stock for 40 years is a nice game to be good at". People that have the right mind-set toward money and wealth always think long-term. Even if they act as though they're just doing everyday operations, they have a masterplan that covers a long period of time, with intermediate steps and check points. If you want to get rich, the blueprint for it covers your entire life and even further. Building a legacy for your off-spring or simply giving it all away can be a rewarding thought that will help you enjoy the process of piling it up.

THE ACT OF INVESTING: AGAIN WHAT IT IS

There are no better words to start with than these ones:

"Investing is laying out money now to get more money back in the future-more money in real terms, after taking inflation into account".
Warren Buffett

This is from an article in Fortune Magazine from November 22nd, 1999. The article was written by Carole Loomis but Buffett reviewed it and added other thoughts you should definitely read over multiple times.
Now, the best way to get more money in the future is to buy something that will produce money now and in the future. Sure enough. A business produces money. But be careful. It must produce significantly more money than all that is needed to keep it alive. Not only it must cover all the costs of

operations, but also all the costs of the structure, plants, and equipment it needs to produce money. It has to have other characteristics too to be a good business, but we will get into that later on.

We have two ways to make an intelligent investment (that is to buy a good business that produces money): buy the entire business (or a very significant stake) if available (and rarely it is at a very good price) or buy a piece of this same business through the medium of marketable securities. For the sake of simplicity, we consider "common stocks "as marketable securities because they entitle us to dividends, voting rights and the most profit if the business grows in value.

Now, let's come back to the characteristics of our intelligent investment. We are buying it with a long-term vision, for the most profit and to stay safe at the same time. Safe means "safer" than the other opportunities available at the same time. It also means, in Graham's words, that "can ensure the safe of the principal"(eventually and hopefully). So, before writing about how to evaluate its "Intrinsic Value" and compare it to its price, first we want to make sure we are dealing with a business we can understand and that its worth the time of our evaluation. And hopefully we try to search for a very good or wonderful business. Why not? Don't be in a hurry. Nothing is forcing us to act immediately or in accordance to a strict deadline. So, let's give it a try.

THE TEST

Just what are the characteristics of a business that meet Buffet's test, deeming it a good candidate to buy?
As I said, nothing is better than his own words:

"It has to be a business that I understand. It has to be a company that I think has some kind of enduring competitive advantage. It has to be a management that I like and trust and it has to be at a reasonably attractive price. Price is the least important but it's still important. And I'd like to own all of it but not necessarily"

The approach of thinking like a business owner and pretending to buy a company in its entirety is crucial to the "Intelligent Investor". It enables and trains him to have a different mind-set than that of a stock speculator. This unique blueprint will guide him through the selecting and sifting process of the investment universe before taking the decision to enter into his new venture. With this approach in mind, you will rarely be tempted to indulge in analyzing businesses that are far from meeting the test requirements.

A BIRD IN THE HAND

Every business is worth the present value (the sum you are ready to lay out now) of all the cash that it will disgorge in perpetuity. Buffett says that if it was possible to know all the streams of cash flow that the business will generate year after year, from now to judgement day, this number would be a precise figure. But, even if it is not a precise number, it can be a roughly precise number, if we can apply an adequate margin of safety. There can be many ways to establish a margin of safety, one is for sure to take into consideration the amount of capital (or equity) required to obtain the streams of cash flow. This is a kind of cornerstone for me. I've been doing more than well owning a business with a high margin of gain compared to the capital involved. I appreciate the strength and durability of such a business, especially during hard times.

Remember that we are looking to acquire a business for less than what is worth, or for much less than what it is worth. So a disparity between our calculations and its actual price could make the buy interesting and profitable. We are looking to buy two birds in a bush while giving away the bird we have in our hand. Fair enough, but be careful! We are, like Aesop in 600 BC, missing something we can't miss as "intelligent investors": when am I going to get the two birds in the bush, and what is the present interest rates?

Buffett says that if Aesop would have followed those 2 factors, "he would have defined investment for the next 2600 years". To do this in practice it is not as easy as it is to explain. Buffett knows most of the time how to predict and evaluate the future cash flow of a business; how to make a precise evaluation of how much is convenient to spend today to buy it. This is a particular twist on all the good principles of value investing he learnt from Graham. It's what he calls the "earning power" of the business. I think his ability to evaluate the earning power of a business and focus on that more than Graham or Schloss did, comes from his particular and peculiar way of navigating through some aspects of accounting. Forget about him having a formula, a precise pattern, or path that he constantly uses for every 10K or 10Q or financial report. No. It's not from a single 10K or especially a single 10Q that drives his prediction. It's from an entire framework. Firstly, he uses filters to sift through the main data and characteristics of the company. Secondly, in applying his vision of the high or low earning horse powers of the business engine he wants to evaluate, Buffett adjusts or substitutes some items based upon the peculiarity of the company. He does that for the now, the past, and the future. Now, the future is always unpredictable but the past is irreversible and, in some cases, he goes back very far. Like with Coca-Cola, he went back to the birth of the company. Amazing. Every piece of financial data, news, numbers, and statistics he could have at hand were there for reading and studying. He wasn't focusing on the short-term. And buying 400 million shares of Coke, it wasn't for the short term. He got a high-profit, indeed.

DON'T FORGET INFLATION AND INTEREST RATES

Inflation is never a good thing. If we have to adjust all things to inflation it means that a good level of inflation is zero. As low as possible is a foregone conclusion. I would disagree with any other opinion about inflation. But the real key factor that impacts our valuations in investing is interest rates. They are the gravity force against which we must compare our rate of return, wanted or expected. Remember: the more the interest rates go up, the more they drive down all kinds of evaluation, stocks included. You have to buy stocks at the lowest price of value to get the same results as before. Even if the change is immediately recognizable in bonds, the ripple effect is less obvious but equally evident in everyone's loan, mortgage, or outstanding debt and therefore affects the value of a farm, a building, houses and so on. In relation to your stock buying, you don't need to know a lot more than this. Grab anything you can on the subject, which is always an implicitly good piece of advice, but again to fight inflation you need more than ever to own a good company. You must have a business that can rise the prices without losing momentum. If you are the best game in town, you can do that. You also can revise the cost-structure and cut some costs. But that is more difficult to do and sometimes even dangerous.

THE MORE THE BETTER BUT STAY SIMPLE

The more you read and learn, the better off you are. But in the end, stay simple. Above all remember not to forget the basic principles at the moment you need them most. Remember the appropriate principles to increase your chances of recalling the right thing to do at the right time. I would also apply this rule of thumb when it comes to analyzing a company. Don't make it too simple. Natural and typical it is not. But make it as easy as possible. If you add too many variables and "bullet points" to your thinking, it's likely you'll make more mistakes. ***You need to focus on what's important. Focus on the key-variables of the business***, the company you understand. Don't cause yourself confusion, stay simple. Jump 6 inches hurdles, if you can. I'm not saying I'm against long check-lists or accurate investigations. They are two different animals. If you feel you need to investigate more it is excellent if you do. But don't do that to build more "theory". Instead find more facts about the company. It's the only thing that will help you. But also remember what Graham wrote in "Security Analysis": the analyst can't be right every time.

GROWTH AND VALUE

If you have been a business owner and if you really have a business mind, you will not see any difference between growth and value. Growth stock or Value stock? The question itself is inappropriate. Such distinction doesn't exist in real terms. If I buy a piece of a business for far below what it is worth, it's because I expect the Market will sooner or later adjust the price of the stock to the same level as the cash flow that the business produces. I expect this cash flow to grow in the long term. This growth will certainly increase the intrinsic value of the business overall. When a company becomes fashionable, the price of stocks will far exceed the present value of the business and will cause there to be high expectation of future earnings. So they called the stock a "growth stock", because the price is increasing but in reality, the intrinsic value of the company is still the same. The decision you are making is still a "value decision": "I predict that this business will be of more value in the future". To assume a business is more valuable just because the price of its stocks is rising is simply asinine. The problem with most traders and naïve speculators is that they are making this bet unconsciously. Growth, if any, is part of the value. They are part of the same equation. I may consider paying a premium on top of the intrinsic value of a business that seems to have more potential than another equal or similar business. It may be for many reasons (I see more value in the management, in the products, it is better positioned, it has a stronger brand... so on and so forth) but in the end, it is always a "value decision". Therefore, there's no such thing as "Value" stocks VS "Growth" stocks.

This is one of the topics in my one-to-one course that stimulates the most interesting conversations.

ADAPTING BOOK VALUE TO MODERN TIMES

We mentioned the importance of book value for investors like Graham and Schloss. If you have assets, and we assume dependable assets (their value is more than what the company is selling for), it's like you're buying an on-going business for nothing. Free. It's not a wishful thinking that this approach works with a group of similar securities and relatively small amounts of investment money; it holds both the future possibility of profit and a high margin of safety.

When Buffett was working for Graham in the early fifties, sitting in his office in New York near his chief analyst "Big Walt" Schloss, his approach was entirely similar. But some years later, the book value turned into a starting point. A consideration of some utility, sure enough, but it had taken a secondary role with the passing of time. Until in 1995, Buffett stated that its importance (in comparison with other characteristics) had significantly diminished. Let's hear from him what I transcribed from that 1995 meeting. A word of caution: I still read some books about "Buffett Accounting" that allegedly state how important it is for Buffett that the book value remains under 1.0, how critical this ratio is and so forth. I cringe every time I see it. It's not only pretentious to write a book on how Buffett regards accounting, but many conclusions are completely inaccurate. Evidently the authors didn't take the time to listen to the shareholders meetings and glean more wisdom directly from Buffett's own words. We are not going to make the same mistake:

"Book Value virtually is not a consideration at all. The best businesses by definition are going to be businesses that earn very high returns on capital employed over time.

By nature, if we want to own good businesses, we are going to own things that have relatively little capital employed compared to our purchase price. That would not be Ben Graham's approach. But Ben was not working with very large sums of money and he would have not argued with this approach, he just would have said it was easier, perhaps when you are working with small amounts of money.

My friend Walter Schloss has hued much more toward the kind of securities that Ben would have selected but he has worked with small amounts of money; he has an absolutely sensational record; and it's not surprising to me at all. When Walter left Graham and Newman, I would expect him to do well but I don't look at the primary message from our standpoint of Graham really has been in anything to do with formulas."

This message truly reflects the aspects that we study in our three sections. If you stay with them and they resonate with you, you can then change, adjust, update and diversify or not. But **the key aspects are inside of you** and will lead you to do well in stocks. No matter what approach you use. It will take time. Be patient, because time is the friend of good principles and good people. I would also add what Buffett said in another shareholders meeting where legendary investor

Phil Carret was present. I will never be tired of repeating those key-aspects: when you have the right attitude and temperament towards the market you are already ahead of 90 percent of other players in the market. If you think like a business-owner regarding your common stocks decision, patience will do all the rest. Learn from Phil Carret.

THERE IS NO SECRET TO INVESTING

When I occasionally come across books about investing with titles like "subtleties" or "secrets" or books alluding to something very sophisticated on how to allocate capital, I always frown. The same feeling arises when I hear certain theories on how to build or structure a portfolio. Unfortunately, Deltas, Betas and other intricacies are common when teaching investing. As common as they are useless. You don't need a formula or a spreadsheet to intelligently allocate capital. Nonetheless many prefer to abandon some of their common sense or business skills and pay high fees when it comes to utilizing their money. Seemingly smart business owners simply give up too soon and stop focusing when money starts piling up in their accounts. The most common mistake: the misallocation of capital. They start to overspend or buy things for no reason. Then, they start trading or gambling just because it is fun or entertaining and so lose capital. Sometimes they also try to expand their business in areas they don't understand well or where they don't have any real advantage over the competition. Real estate is one of the most popular play-grounds. The management and directors of Coca-Cola also made some of these mistakes back in the 80s, such as investing poorly the extra-cash available. I made this mistake myself when I bought an investment property just for vending machines. I was not an expert in vending machines. I learnt a hard lesson. I didn't have the right attitude, I didn't say 'NO 'to myself. I wouldn't admit to myself that I didn't have the skills or experience to estimate the value of the business, the depreciation, or the salvation value of the machines. Last but not the least, I didn't use an adequate margin of safety to save me from all this. And even if I had, the first two errors would have killed me anyway. If you overpay for something, there are few or no ways to fix that.

One take away from this paragraph is that essentially the notion of how to think outside of the box or go against the crowd is extremely crucial. It's true that according to human nature, it is justifiable to fail and lose money in a conventional way but absolutely unacceptable to lose the same amount in a new, unfashionable way. If everybody does it, you don't blame yourself because you lose the same as everyone else. Don't start your journey in the investment world like that. You will learn from your mistakes, but if you can learn from mista-kes of others, that's even better.

BUY MONEY

Buying businesses is the quintessence of investing. A good business produces money under the form of "Net Income" or "Retained Earnings" that can be reinvested intelligently. If you want a "secret recipe", it is all in these two lines. The less capital it takes to obtain the "secret recipe", the better the business. The more consistent it is in repeating the same "recipe" on its menu, the better. Think about Coca-Cola, Ferrari, McDonalds, Starbucks, Disney. Stick with what works, repeat and expand.

OBSERVE, MEASURE AND QUANTIFY BUT IN THE END ITS MORE LIKE PAINTING

You can measure, you can quantify. You can evaluate the tangible assets, gauge the value of the brand, the qualities of managers, their stories and integrity or devotion to the company. And if you don't, forget it. But remember it's not just about being good in math or calculations. The numbers are just more colors to add to a "story" of the company and the business. Feel more like a painter, an artist than an assessor or technician. Even if you are a competent CPA, when it comes to investing you are more of a thinker, an artist painting a vision. A landscape of the future.

It is true that as much as you feel detached from the possibilities of making measurements or assessments, you have to be careful. But don't expect to be a scientist. You are more an explorer. The true investor sometimes can be more like Columbus and have the same qualities and traits. **Sometimes the investor is so wrong is right.**

SPECULATION

Don't fool yourself into thinking you are still investing when you are probably being drawn away into speculation. So as long as you know that it is almost impossible not to fall into some form of speculation every once in a while, let's review very briefly what an investment IS NOT. It's the best way to remain in charge of our intentions, desires and rationality. If we do so, we will probably engage in some profitable, intelligent, and not so risky forms of speculation.

INTELLIGENT SPECULATION

I started my first business at 6 years old; I rented vintage Ferraris to imaginary customers willing to pay me from the cash I'd printed myself. I had a 250 GT SWB, a BB512i – a couple of 308 GTB in my "garage" on the shelf near my bed. I put a big red sign and big prancing horse on the shelf. And so it all began.
It was 1982 and I planned to buy a real one for myself one day. It took me 31 years of patience and in 2013 the dream came true.

There is a study (I got this from Buffett) that recently linked successful business minds to the age at which they had their first business. But consistency wins. I in fact followed all the price fluctuations of every vintage Ferrari model for 31 years, until in 2013, when prices were at their lowest level ever, I bought one. It was not an investment. Be careful. Even though you may hear from many Ferrari's owners that it is, they only think so because they saw the price going up. You are now almost a "professional". Don't fall into the trap. If emotions are largely involved in determining the price, you are not investing. Having said that, let's see if it can be an intelligent speculation. Let's move from our "Value" cornerstones that consider the "Value" we get in relation to the price we are asked to pay. First and foremost, it was a pleasure to buy it due to sweet memories, happy emotions, and affordability (my net worth and cash flow at the time allowed for the purchase). Plus, I had thought that maintenance would cost me more than it actually does. So, I used a margin of safety, combined with low-expectations of its yearly costs and figured out that I could afford it eventually. Plus, there's nothing wrong in buying happiness at a reasonable price every once in a while, if it is within your means and makes you feel like a kid again. It will create some positive ripple effects around you and help you be thankful for what you have and do more to be sure you deserve it. Guess what happened next: in the following 8 years the "Ferrari Index" sky-rocketed, driving up the price of every vintage model and breaking records at auctions. Now I will never sell happiness, but eventually this "non-investment" and unintentional speculation that doubled in price was certainly a smart move. It was based on a principle that must be second nature for every "Value Investor", even when he is not investing: never overpay for anything.

I will repeat it again as a caveat: don't fool yourself. On such rare occasions you do something like that, you are not investing. Limit doing this as much as possible. You have expertise in a field (art, vintage cars, watches, antique trade) and you can assess the correct price of something beautiful that you are sure is not a fake. The money locked in that expensive frame or toy will not produce anything more than emotions and a sensation of "bello" (beauty in Italian). But "bello" can make you happy; happiness and freedom are sometimes worth exchanging for money. Do it intelligently with your eyes open.

GOLD AND COMMODITIES ARE NOT INVESTING

Gold doesn't produce anything. Nickel can be considered very precious for its multiple tech applications. Platinum too. They are useful and you can successfully exploit some price fluctuations from the market. Be aware. That is a speculative attitude. It is not real investing. If you feel you can make some money off those metals, I wouldn't argue with you. But from my perspective, a true investor doesn't waste time and money on those activities. I never did and I suppose I never will.

Let's also do some math in favor of the 'intelligent investor'. If in 1942, you had put 10,000 dollars on the entire S&P 500 (even though at the time there were no index funds available), today you would have 51 million dollars at your disposal. The production of businesses in America as a whole was so huge and powerful. Just betting on America. If you had put the same 10k dollars on gold, you would have today roughly 470,000 dollars. 51 million versus half a million is a huge difference.

Also add all the efforts and expenses needed to protect your 10k dollars of gold for so long (80 years) and store it properly. While I'm writing this, there is a show on a famous American TV Channel with many "famous" talking heads of the investment worlds. They are suggesting that common people be afraid of the rising inflation and protect themselves. How? By putting your money into gold. Let me echo Charlie Munger: "A civilized person doesn't invest his money in gold". Let me further add a personal note: "just like a gentleman doesn't embellish his appearance with a chain of gold around his neck".

SO I SOLD GOLD TO BUY A STOCK THAT DOESN'T LOVE ME

Forget about the name "stock". Call it a "piece of a business". You don't own "stocks", you own a claim of assets, intangibles and you have employees. Feel like you are paying their W2, their payroll check with your investment. Feel like you are one of the owners and so you want to prosper and stay as long as you can in the business. Observe your investment by looking at the business, not its stocks and its everyday fluctuations. Be rational, that means always be ready to measure and quantify. Those two verbs must stay inside your head as a mantra. Measure and quantify, but remember it is not enough. Use your judgement, don't fall in love with your measurements. And don't fall in love with stocks. They don't love you. Again, it's about temperament, as it is explored in the first section, and it is so critical that can undermine your technical skills. Don't fall in love with any business. Businesses don't care about you and they don't know who you are. We are passionate about business; we care about the people that made them possible and turned them into outstanding companies. People are the ones that make them profitable and useful. Use your reasoned choice about businesses because we want to be loved back by human beings, not by pieces of a business. We don't dream of being loved back by a stock. We don't take stocks out to dinner on a date. So be ready to use them for the good of human beings, society, and yourself. With the stock market, you have a tremendous advantage: the ability of selling portions of, or your entire participation in a business. That is, if you wish to do so and if it fits with your book and your circumstances. Don't let any emotional bond dictate your willingness to buy or sell a business you like. Do what makes sense to you and serves you well financially. You can rearrange your little basket of businesses you own in a

click or two. You can always apply the principle of "opportunity cost" in selling something to buy something else if it is
more attractive. It's a possibility that wasn't available to the
old business owners in the steel industry, oil or mines and it
is still not available to the controlled businesses that are not
quoted publicly. Take advantage of what Graham called the
"double status".

THE DOUBLE STATUS

I made my first money in real estate. I was already passionate about stocks, Ben Graham, and Buffett but I had very
little money to invest. Nonetheless, I started with 100 bucks
and found a job as a "sales associate" in a famous real estate
brokerage firm. My first good idea was to have an income
that I would underspend. It's not necessary to start with a
large amount of money. You don't need a high income to
do well. It's more about how you manage what you save. I
worked and studied a lot in 2005 to be licensed as a broker.
In Italy, it's a demanding, 6-month course, but education
almost always pays off in the short and long term. When my
income increased, I was part of the real estate business, I had
a couple of years in which I poorly allocated my hard-earned capital. I bought some investment properties that had a
return on equity that is still considered very poor compared
to the usual performance of my stock portfolio. I was trying

to find my real self in investing and learning. You hear a lot of things, you read a lot of different books and publications, TV headlines, etc...;it is not easy at the beginning. I've been in your shoes (that's why I'm writing this book and decided to pass along what I learnt). Then I finally found my true passion in common stocks. My dream of finally owning multiple businesses came true when I started purchasing common stocks thinking about them as pieces of business, and acting like I owned the entire company.

Investing in stocks gives you benefits you cannot find in real estate. It's the "double status" that Graham describes when talking about the share holder of marketable securities. Unlike other investments, in RE for instance, you are not only the owner of a piece of a company that has a value in relation to its balance sheet and earning power. You are in an extremely key position that enables you to sell all or even just a portion of the ownership at your disposal. You don't need lots of documents, titles, notary public or exhausting negotiations. . You don't need to fight with workers; you are not trying to win at the game of flipping houses for a quick profit and the renovation is going very slowly.

With stocks you are hands off. You are the owner of a piece of a business or multiple businesses. You can own a lot of them if you so choose, and you can re-arrange your basket of properties in the blink of an eye. You can do it at a price that is there to serve you and you can agree with it or not at your convenience. Mr. Market can be your obliging partner in this way, every day. You don't have to put in all the effort, time, risk, and capital that is required to make huge profit, like in flipping houses. You can manage the amount of money involved and even decide when and where to stop if things don't go as planned or how you wanted them to. And most of all, you can thrive and earn so much more with even just a single shrewd decision made in the stock market. In order to achieve this goal, you have to change your way of thinking when comes to stocks. Let's see how and why.

BUSINESS EVALUATION VS MARKET EVALUATION

The advantage and the possibility of selling or buying more of the business you own must entice you to refine your skills and experience in evaluating businesses. In fact, only focusing on the key variables and strengths of a company, assessing a number, an almost precise estimate of the business you own will put you in an extremely advantageous position in exploiting the fluctuations of price that only the stock market can give you.

Always remember that Mr. Market, with his mood swings, is there to serve you, not to instruct you. You have to be informed as well as you can be about the business or businesses you own. You never expect Mr. Market to inform you. You let the market be your servant.

Many examples in the past taught us that the stock market can be very wrong in predicting the real value of the under-

lying business and its prospects. It's your duty to stay informed, prepared, alert and
courageous enough to take advantage of the disparity betwe-
en your estimate and Mr. Market's estimate of what's going
on with your business.

*"The Investor need not watch his companies performance like a
hawk; but he should give it a good, hard look from time to time"*
BEN GRAHAM (chapter 8 pag.203 "The intelligent Investor")

This is one of Ben Graham's statements that I've been on bo-
ard with since the beginning of my journey. It was useful and
comforting to know that I didn't need to be a hawk. It all see-
med doable, even if I felt naïve and a rookie at the time. After
many years, I know from experience that it was doable and
it served me very well. It may easily happen, if you are lucky
enough to find a wonderful business, (one you understand,
with good prospects and at an attractive price), that you will
end up owning as many shares of it as possible. It may happen it will be 38% of your portfolio. Yes, almost 40% with a
single stock. This is my situation right now and I'm happy with
it. You'll certainly need to give it a good, hard, look from time
to time. As true investors, we will work together throughout
my one-to-one course to learn how to read a 10K, how help
your company thrive, and who its competitors are now and
even 10-15 years from now. It will help you a lot in following
the vicissitudes of your business, keep your judgement up-to-

date, and give you a platform based on facts. Following these steps, you'll eventually feel ready to predict if your business is undervalued or overvalued and how to play the difficult game of buying low and selling high.

THE TRUE INVESTOR

The temporary and excessive considerations of Mr. Market are the ones you want to exploit for the most success. Buffett has been a master at doing this, and he's certainly learnt a lot from chapter 8 of "The Intelligent Investor". He considered it when buying American Express in the sixties (in the middle of a scandal due to fraud for nonexistent provisions), Geico (the first and second time at least), and the Washington Post in the early seventies.

The true investor never sells or feels forced to sell because the price of his stocks are going down. The true investor never buys or feels compelled to buy because the price of his stocks are going up.

The true investor usually does what the crowd is not doing and acts only upon his own conclusions and judgement of the present and future value of the business. Unjustified market fluctuations or vagaries are only useful to him if he can take advantage of them or of the outlandishly low or high price of the stocks, in terms of "Value".

The true investor acts as though he owns the entire company. That is his approach. He stays in the business through the good and bad times, as long as he can see the sun shining in the future. He sometimes thinks about the future or may be concerned about what is happening at the moment. It's human. But rationality and a vision for the distant future must always prevail over emotions. A business owner has persistence and wisdom. He is ready to own his piece of a business for 10, 20, 30 or more years. He is able to judge if his company is still robust and profitable, even if its stocks or the whole market are plunging for some reason.

He would be delighted to buy more of the company at a discount. He thinks of himself as a net buyer of groceries over the long term. He likes specials and discounts. He wants to eagerly buy things for far below what they are worth.
And that's the only golden rule you will ever have. It will help you survive, and eventually thrive in a sea infested with sharks and the blood of people who jumped in without the proper equipment that you have: a proper attitude, skills and margin of safety.

MR. MARKET, A FUNNY PARTNER

Let's see what kind of other players jump in every day to day-trade in the marketplace.
In 2010, in just 36 minutes, on May the 6th, the Dow Jones lost 998 points. Not a slight fall (at almost ten per cent, in half

an hour). The "flash crash" was supposedly due to the algorithms of machines used nowadays to buy and sell at the speed of light. An aberration, and an attempt of illegal manipulation by some traders adds to the pile of Mr. Market's crazy emotions. It's something we have to face. Human nature, prone to greediness and immediate profit, is and will always remain the same. But on top of that, it seems that we, now, thanks to technology (more like the misuse of it) are allowed to put this poor, heavily drinking, manic-depressive guy at the "wheel of a car", so to speak. And no surprise, for Wall Street, it's no big deal; it's perfectly legal that he drives around on the "highway of capitalism" with only the help of some computer software. Needless to say, it can be dangerous. But what's our main takeaway? I may be wrong, but I suppose by driving in a different lane, the "Value Lane", we are able to take advantage of the folly of machines that were created by the foolishness of men. Technology can be used in a good way to benefit society or in bad way to take short cuts that mean the stock market won't work for everyone. Graham is still right, even after all these decades. Like all "formula plans", it will not work. It just opened the flood gates for manipulators and dishonest traders to modify software to create artificial, unwanted fluctuations and panic. It's dangerous and keeps honest people away from the market.

An intelligent man will always be more efficient than a machine, an algorithm, or a software, in assessing the right "Value of the Market" over the long term. Businesses, as we are just starting to discover, speak a language of numbers, but also have a story and traits that only a man's trained mind can understand and gauge. Mr. Market will be sober and alert again, he is there to serve you. As Graham brilliantly stated, "The market over the short term is a "voting machine"; but over the long term is a "weighing machine" ". And that's what it counts for us. We do believe that it is so, and that it will remain so.

"Ben said just imagine that when you buy a stock, in effect you bought into a business where you have this obliging partner who comes around every day and offers you a price at what you either buy or sell and the price is identical. No one ever gets that in a private business where daily you get a buy/sell offer by a party. But in the stock market you get. That's a huge advantage. And it's a bigger advantage if this partner of yours is a heavy drinking, manic-depressive. The crazier he is, the more money you are going to make. As an investor you love volatility. Nor if you're on margin; but if you're an investor you aren't on margin. If you are an investor you love the idea of wild swings because it means more things are going to get mispriced".

Warren Buffett

Amen.

Now, before wrapping up the second section, let's repeat once more what I really want to stick with you right away.

THINK LIKE A BUSINESS OWNER

The better the business man you are, the better the investor you will be. And vice versa. The two skills are correlative and will help feed and support each other. They go together. For the most outstanding results in stocks, you don't want to think as a stock speculator but as a business owner. I said it again.

All the great successful investors have been in one way or another business owners. Even if only on a small scale. I myself pretended to be a business owner at the age 6. Sitting on my bed, I rented Ferraris to rich customers from a price list that gave me a lot of money (I had printed it myself on pieces of paper). It was my favorite game. Buffett started at a later age, working as a paper boy and trading Coke to his grandpa. Obviously smarter than me since he made real money and not just pieces of paper.

WRITE DOWN THE NUMBERS: YOURS AND YOUR BUSI-NESS'S

If you write things down, they stick with you. You will most likely memorize and have in mind all your own numbers. I suggest you start with your cash flow statement. It's shows in real-time what happens to your money. I heard that J.D. Rockfeller also kept track of the money that came in and went out every day. I always know what is going out and what is coming in and why. Of course, it is beneficial. It gives me the opportunity to sometimes save more or sometimes spend more if I want to. It gives me control of my money. It's very educational and it makes a real difference over the long term in saving more and accumulating wealth. You don't write down receivables, deferred taxes, or expenses, nor the occasional large expense, like buying a house or a car. You want to be sure to keep track of your daily expenditures but record large expenses separately. You will be surprised how smarter spending allows you to save a lot and stockpile money for the future. It's the best form of wealth, one that nobody sees but is there in your bank account. You will use it or increase it, according to your needs. It's another "joy of investing". Remember: you need to save to start investing to be able to get rich. In order to save, you need to underspend your income. You need to know how to cut down and what to cut out to be profitable and well-off. It is not easy; it's easy to spend money, not save it. That is why those who are only good at spending usually go back to being poor, even if they happened to get rich.

HABITS AND EDUCATION
MAKE ALL THE DIFFERENCE

If you are reading this book, you are willing to educate yourself in becoming wealthy and free. That is the difference between you and the majority of people out there. I'm confident you will get there. You'll learn how to safely navigate through difficulties, enabling you to make more and more. Money and savings will bring you the ultimate intangible assets: time and freedom. Independence is the first and most precious reward for those able to save enough to free themselves from fear. Fear of being fired, fear of the future, fear of getting sick and the anxiety that comes from not having enough time for the things you love and the ones you love. Be active in trying to achieve what you love, and start now. Don't care about what others do or think. Start educating yourself about money and investing. **Start as soon as you can. Hang around with lovable, happy people.** You'll be surprised you'll find my direct cell number and email through the internet. I'm here to help. Don't be bashful, Just give me a call.

Section Three:
Margin of Safety

A GOLDEN RULE, EASY TO FORGET

There are many ways to approach the evaluation of a business. As I've already mentioned, two good business minds may arrive at a conclusion that is roughly similar but never exactly the same. The last assessment may be two numbers almost equal to each other, but rarely exactly the same. But I have good news for you. In evaluating a business in order to buy it as a whole, or a part of it through its stocks, you don't have to be very precise. It's impossible. But what you can do (and must do) is to add a margin of safety into your calculations. Always follow the first rule: don't lose. You must try to protect yourself and your investment from any downfalls. To be sure that you are buying a business for far below what it is worth, you should have a wide margin, the wider the better. Now, how to do that is a pretty interesting game to play. It comes with many possible consequences, aspects, and considerations that I explain in detail in my course. It is something that I barely touched on in section two of this book. It requires a flexible and prudent mind, accustomed to thinking through the consequences of everything before doing it. It is useful for life in general. It is a calculation but it's more of an art than a science. It is like what happens in the insurance underwriting process. Will it really work? Only time will tell. We simply must do everything we can to ensure that it does. It doesn't matter much if you use a margin of safety for the "reduced rate" of future cash flows or if you use the same margin in forecasting the same streams of future cash flows. Or with both. Or if you are more skilled at evaluating the assets of a company and their salvation value in case of bankruptcy, or something of that sort. Each of us has their own background and adventures in business that will unavoidably lead him to do better in one sector or another. You know what you know; use this knowledge and expertise to better evaluate where to safely place the margin. The only thing you don't want to do is to forget about it. Don't hit the road without securing your load; don't cross the bridge without checking that your load is way less heavy than the maximum weight allowed.

"Here the function of the Margin of Safety is, in essence, that of rendering unnecessary an accurate estimate of the future".

Ben Graham, the Intelligent Investor (Chapter 20)

I intentionally underlined "accurate".
Buffett is a master at applying Graham's concept and he also added his own twist and special skills to it. He started to master the concept many years ago when, for a patient investor, there were more undervalued opportunities available. He underpaid so much for See's Candy, Geico, and the Washington Post that over the next decades, he made the outstanding, breathtaking gains for which he is famous, and rightly so. He saw that the potential of those businesses, combined

with a very low price would ensure a wider margin of safety to his purchase. He felt that the price gave him some protection from risk and not the other way around (the famous bet taught in business schools that a higher volatility increases the risk!). An ordinary student of Buffett and Graham would look at the business, its debt, and fundamentals and would ponder carefully before writing down on a piece of paper a number at which he would buy, with a margin of safety, the entire company. Then, the process of buying starts. It may go quickly or slowly. It could take a 'New York minute' or continue for years. But as Buffett brilliantly pointed out during a shareholders meeting: if the price of the stock goes even lower than our estimate, could somebody rationally explain to me why the deal becomes riskier and not safer (since it provides me with a wider margin of safety)?

EARNING POWER

Through the years, Buffett used his ability of applying a margin of safety to attractive or (more recently) "reasonably attractive" priced investments, and added his own particular twist to it by reducing at a "Present Value" the future streams of the business's cash flow. This quality, that we also call the "earning power" of a business, is mainly based on his vast experience of evaluating past earnings and projecting what they'll be in the future. He does that by considering the intrinsic characteristics of a business. Those traits become part of his value judgement. They add or don't add value to the calculation of the "conventional" intrinsic value. All this combined with his shrewd talent for evaluating the managers of a company (a quality absent in Walter Schloss) made him into a killer investor. Another thing to remember, he almost never acts instantaneously: he read about the prospect of the Washington Post in 1971. Then, in 1973 he bought its stocks when something caused them to plunge far below their book value. He also hit the nail on the head with his evaluation of the integrity and potential of Katherine Graham and the Graham family as owners-managers. Working together brought about incredible results. This pattern of success repeated over and over for 6 decades until the last good deal: Apple. He waited for years to understand a business that he considered completely new to him. Then he learnt that it was not so new for his business mind. He figured out the potential it had with all its wonderful economics and products. He has experience in knowing what goes on in a consumer's mind. And needless to say, he knows how good a manager like Tim Cook is. All in all, a smash hit.

A SIMPLE IDEA, A LOT TO DISCOVER

Let's get back to the heart of the "Margin of Safety". It is indeed so simple. But to get to the third step of the process, that is to act and put it in practice, is another story.
Graham, Buffett, and Schloss can really help us if we have the patience to carefully pay attention to their instructions; if

we are able to read between the lines and contemplate their crystal-clear reasoning. They had different methods of staying safe but they were all based on the same idea: Graham's "The Margin of safety".

Can a common stock be as safe as a corporate bond? Could it still be safe when considering its "principal" (the capital) involved? For Graham, the answer is a possible "yes". By applying some of safety measures that I explain in my course, you can maintain all the possible up-sides of a common stock, while having an appropriate margin of safety on the down-side. How to properly execute this safer method I cover in detail during my one-to-one lessons. Yet again, it is about sifting through the numbers regarding what the business owns and what the business is worth. Its future earning power and its growth are all "value decisions" and evaluations to take into consideration. So, if it's true that the method can be carried over into the field of common stocks, it is also true that some necessary modifications are required
(as Graham himself warns us). We do not have time or space to go into that more here.

P/E IS JUST A STARTING POINT (BUT NOT A JOKE)

The title of this paragraph says it all. Again, it's so simple but that's also why it's so difficult. In my one- on-one lessons, I point out some key considerations for analyzing price over earnings. I know it is debatable, but I clearly know that "price" is what I pay and "value" is what I get. If searching for "Value" is my main goal, my strategy is to never overpay for anything, anywhere, at any time. There's no way to fix it if you have already paid too much for something. On Buffett's list of characteristics for a business, the price may be the least important factor but "it is still important".

We would concur with Graham that the price is probably the most secure margin of safety, once you have made sure that the issue isn't so large that it requires you walk away. In my course, we dig into some useful data and statistics of P/E, including the P/E of the S&P 500 over the last century. There are many lessons to be learnt there.

2 KEY POINTS TO BEAR IN MIND

Two key points to bear in mind while looking for the margin of safety are:

1. The positive one: once you found a wonderful business to buy into, be ready to add more to what you have if the price enables you to apply your calculation or re-calculation of the margin. If the price goes down substantially, buying more can be safer than looking for other opportunities that may seem more attractive for the price, but aren't as strong of a business.

2. The negative one: avoid major risk. Don't buy something

that is speculative in nature, such as buying a business for a reduced price but has no competitive advantage or solid brand, and above all has weak economics and no chance of growing or fixing its problems. A lousy past almost always guarantees that a luminous future is just not going to happen. Just walk away. It's one thing to be temporary depressed or troubled due to the vicissitudes that can occur during the lifetime of a good business. It's another to be weak in nature.

PUT A MARGIN IN YOUR LIFE

"There is no dignity quite so impressive, and no independence quite so important, as living within your means."

Calvin Coolidge

Why did I include in "the Margin of Safety" section an old-fashioned quote from the 30th president of the United States? Because if you want your money to grow, you have to save it and know how to invest it appropriately. That's what we are here. Underspending your income is the first step. At the beginning, it could mean living at least within or even below your means. If you have a gameplan and your goal is clear (buying undervalued stocks), temporarily living under your means could not only be acceptable but also very educational. Not only will you feel like a stoic philosopher, a descendant of Seneca or Marcus Aurelius, but you will also put a solid margin of safety on your financial future. You will pick up a habit. And the longer you apply this habit of a margin of safety on your financial life, the more you will be able to grow rich and independent in the future. I know it may seem repetitive to mention it all the time, but you may have to give up something today for a bigger reward tomorrow. It's the bird in the hand for two birds in the bush. But instead of complaining, you are here reading this third section because you've already read the first section about temperament. You've learnt how to enjoy the process. You would actually love to give up something today to get more tomorrow. You are doing it with a smile and immediately feeling a sense of gratification. If you are capable of thinking independently, you know what is the best and most rewarding road for you to follow to gain financial success. You are acquiring the mindset of a billionaire, not a millionaire. You are achieving a habit that will stay with you when you are rich, and it will make you even richer. You will have more without becoming a slave to: "I need to make more", just to pay for things you buy to impress people. Don't go there. Remember: "The best way to achieve something is to deserve it". Be ready to be disciplined. Be ready to work hard and do the extra-work. Becoming rich just to impress people is the fastest way to return to poverty. If you were to actually act like a rich person, then you will do this knowing it is for your freedom. It will enable you to do whatever you want, whenever you want, without having to ask anyone for permission (especially your wallet or even worse somebody's else wallet). Enjoying your independence will allow you to work on things that you like. This will make you even happier and wiser. Be respectful of this privilege. It's a huge achievement that few people have the luck, strength and capability of acquiring. So, deserve it. Be respectful of money, don't squander it.

SPEND WISELY

Living within your means or under, in proportion to your newly acquired wealth, will be more impressive than getting a new boat or a big house. There is no such dignity or setting of a good example as outstanding as that. You will be safe and independent; this is so important in making you feel happy and confident of every new investment decision. You'll be like Buffett. Listen to Silent Cal Coolidge. Show your strength! You are not a miser at all, you are giving yourself the privilege of having a high inner score card. Don't worry, soon you will be able to treat yourself to anything you'd like; before "having" you did the hard work of "being". You educated yourself in what it really means to have money. You don't need to show off, you are rich for real. So do so! Put the money intelligently to work for you. Spend it for your pleasure wisely. You were born to be wise. Put that margin of safety on your life and the lives of your loved ones.

APPLICABILITY OF THE MARGIN

The "Margin of safety" has a wider applicability as a key element in all business decisions. Every investment decision is a "Value" decision and conclusion. You can come to a conclusion in many different ways but a margin of safety should always be a part of your last conclusion and assessment.

The "Margin of safety" is also a key element for any intelligent speculation and for any purchase that pertains to a gain in value or an assessment of the salvation value. In my course, I go into much more detail in analyzing the three elements that I find paramount to this process.

I also try to answer a very good question: "Does a wide "Margin of Safety" win over "Diversification" or "Hyper-diversification"?"

CIGAR BUTTS

When Buffett started his professional carrier working for Graham-Newman in New York in 1951, he was looking for what he called "cigar butts". Companies whose stocks were so depressed that the price seem to reflect them as not very good businesses, but sometimes selling so low that still they had a "free puff" left. By managing small amounts of money, he was able to actively make a good profit from rummaging the floor of capitalism in search of cigar butts. They were soggy and ugly but almost free. Many years later when he was dealing with more money, he admitted that the practice is "wrong" if you want to get very rich. Or at least it is impossible when investing large amounts of money. The most interesting thing about studying Warren Buffett is figuring out how his investment style and procedures changed over time.

The main difference between Ben Graham and Warren Buffett in relation to the "Margin of Safety" is "pricing". For Warren, the price is not "low enough" to create a substantial "Margin of Safety" if the business doesn't pass the test of being a good business. If it's not a business he understands and with a competitive durable advantage, there's no price attractive enough anymore, like it was back in the days of the "cigar butts" purchases.

For us regular guy not investing billions all at once, there are still ways to work out investments using something close to the "cigar butt" technique. But we need a correct interpretation of the "Margin of Safety" correlative to other elements. It can be a 'new art' for us to update, adapt and apply to some "modern" companies we understand, the good old principles of "Value Investing". If you deal with small amounts of money, you will still be able to find opportunities even though aren't as many as there were in the past. BUT:

They must be regarded as a speculative events or special occasions and not strictly investing. At least not for the very long term.

However, they can turn into intelligent speculations, when the diligent and careful analyst makes sure he is still taking advantage of a disparity between the price and value of the underlying business he is considering to buy.

NEVER GAMBLE

The "intelligent investor" also uses the "Margin of Safety" as a reminder. He never gambles or overpays for a stock. He is ready to candidly admit that no enterprise is totally risk free. And so is every stock purchase. But he always does the best he can to calculate the odds in his favor (also in speculative actions). Above all, he limits the number of these operations as much possible to zero.

PERMANENT HOLDINGS

If he has enough money, he will look for businesses he's confident will last and be profitable forever. Enough money means that he will not have to sell a good business to buy another one that he values even more or has equally good economics. Be aware, he is not applying any diversification. In this case he is taking advantage of buying more of "something of value". He could "buy back" and add more to what he already has (as we've already said), but only if the price makes sense. If the price of what he already holds as permanent is high, he can refrain from adding more shares or selling. He can turn to a new attractive project without selling the wonderful business he owns. Time is another "margin of safety" you can use in your favor. Time is usually your friend, timing or forecasting are not.

DIVERSIFICATION AS A MARGIN OF SAFETY

We, as investors, will struggle with two dilemmas when it comes to applying a 'margin of safety'.

1. DIVERSIFICATION as a margin of safety
2. PRICE as a margin of safety

Those dilemmas will come up in what we can call "unconventional investments".
I further explain in my course what I consider conventional and unconventional investments and why they are not speculations if they imply, contain, or include a margin of safety.
It is impossible for me to sum up in just a few lines what I learnt from Graham and Buffett as a student when I read the book for the first time almost 20 years ago. But some rules and key concepts that have always helped me and many other value investors are literally gold.

"Investment is most intelligent when it is most business-like"
Ben Graham

It would take not only an entire course but an entire lifetime to sharpen your skills and practice this rule. It will take all the qualities of these three sections combined to invest and think like a business owner and not like a stock speculator.

It always amazes me how efficient and successful business owners cease to think like business owners when it comes to picking out stocks of a good business. They think it is a good thing to treat stocks in a way they never would with their own restaurant, factory, or construction business. In my lessons, I talk about the 4 principles that will help you tremendously in every business field. And investing in stocks is no different than thinking, selecting, and acting like a business man. Investing in stocks is about if, when, and under which circumstances to buy pieces of a business. Because that's what stocks are: pieces of a business.

I established 4 principles during my journey to become a true investor or a more intelligent one.

In my course, you'll discover just how helpful those 4 principles can be if you stick with them your entire investing life. They have to become a part of you and your reasoning. You will know them by heart by the end of the course.

WHAT I DO

I put a "Margin of Safety" on everything. Every calculation I make, every aspect of a business I consider or evaluate, I subsequently go for a low figure. Some times with a wide margin, at other times, with what I think is just slightly below my assessment; it depends on the nature of the business. I usually like the businesses that are not capital intensive. But this is just me and sometimes I make exceptions because of the other outstanding characteristics of some particular business. One example of this is when I bought the stocks of Ferrari (RACE) in 2015 (I explain the reasoning behind it in my course). The most important thing is that you put a margin that makes you safe, and is based upon a measurable, mathematical calculation.

WHAT I DON'T DO

As I've said multiple times, what you don't do is just as important or more important than what you do do. So, I hope you can join me for the entire one-to-one course because in the investment business, this is one of the most interesting and useful things to learn. The stocks you don't buy. And, guess what, it is a subject that nobody talks about. Like nobody that i know tries to teach how to evaluate a company, and what are the key variables and the strenghts of a business and the things that are NOT possible to value. You won't be able to find teachers, professionals, portfolio manager, or even financial planners that are able to articulate much on this subject. The only ones that efficiently taught me how to stay away from disasters were, once again, Ben Graham, Warren Buffett, and Charlie Munger. That's why I've spent almost 20 years sifting through material and meticulously selecting their best pieces of advice about every aspect of investing, money and life. I also have to mention once again Walter Schloss. His adversity to losing money. His integrity. His real sense of responsibility in knowing that he was managing other pe-ople's hard-earned money and savings. His efficient vision to contains his partnership's costs, even when profits were sky-rocketing. His stress on focusing on companies with low debt, and staying safe first on the downside before conside-ring the potentials of the upside. I tried to absorb like a spon-ge every single day those traits and put them to work. They epitomize my attitude toward the market. I describe in detail the three things NOT-TO-DO in my course. They will lead us to safe and beautiful harbors, where we can rest and conti-nue our wonderful journey in search of the "Joy of Investing".

A FINAL WORD

The "Joy of Investing" means real JOY, not just success or winning all the time. You have to enjoy what you do everyday to be happy. So make sure you enjoy what you are doing. You build wealth and financial improvement upon happiness and a sense of fulfillment.

If you are a negative person, or often have negative thoughts, you will waste time, energy and eventually money in looking for something that soon will become impossible for you to achieve. It will be so not because it's impossible in itself but because of your way of thinking.

It can be hard because it is hard and challenging sometimes. It must be so. But if you feel it's taking away too much from you and your good attitude, just take a break and rest. Recharge your batteries and remind yourself to look at the whole picture. Don't give up! You are committed to the end game, patient, and a unique person. Don't be in a hurry. You will find yourself. You will find what works for you. If you stay happy and healthy good things are coming your way. You will win in the end.

REMEMBER: Investing is an art. It's like a flower that you need to water and take care of. This translates to you needing to take care of yourself (body and soul), and your loved ones. It's a simple art but not that simple.

I have no formal training, nor did I finish a business school of any sort. I don't even have a degree. My only "schooling" was studying Ben Graham's two books and everything I found on Buffett. And I can tell there's no more powerful knowledge than the one based upon experience. Over the years, I have found my little shadow under the tree planted by those gentlemen.

And I started from scratch when I was 26 or 27, which isn't that young.

But I FOCUSED and Im DISCIPLINED and I have PERSISTENCE and RESOLUTION. If there's something I want that turns me on, it's like the Ferrari I wanted as a small kid: It can take years but I will succeed. I tried to apply all the rules I learned through the years, especially, the "margin of safety". Sometimes I know I can because I think I can.

I was bad at math at high school and now I study accounting and or read financial reports almost everyday, including Saturdays and Sundays. I always try to "estimate the strength of the entire business" and how much is worth in a very conservative way.

I transcribed a lot of Buffett's public speeches. I wrote down his words and read them over multiple times. If you listen carefully to his speeches, there are a couple of occasions where he gives you some numbers connected to his reasoning that can give you an idea of how his evaluation process works and how he relates one number to another. That in itself is more of an education than any business school or formula could give you, because there is no formula. But you have to listen to him carefully.

"Value Investing" is an inoculation. I hope this book can be that for you: a starting point. The best compliment I could get is that this book is simple. The first step on a long road must be simple. The goal is to keep it simple. But only after you have studied a lot. Doing that, many hours a day, every-day, for years will give you the freedom to keep it as simple as possible. Because in the end, it is never more simple than how it is.

ESSENTIAL BIBLIOGRAPHY

In my opinion, you need to read first and foremost these key books that I list below. And above all, read them multiple times to really absorb and internalize them. They must become a part of you and your entire life. Once you've done that, you will have the tools that enable you to read other books that interest you, make you happy, or add a twist to your established building blocks.

The books to get you through your entire life are:

"THE INTELLIGENT INVESTOR" by Benjamin Graham publisher: Harperbusiness - Revised Edition – Foreword by Warren Buffett

"SECURITY ANALYSIS" by Benjamin Graham and David Dodds publisher: McGraw-Hill Education – 6th edition – Foreword by Warren Buffett

"COMMON STOCKS and UNCOMMON PROFITS" by Philip A. Fisher publisher: Wiley and Sons

"WARREN BUFFETT: The making of an American Capitalist" by Roger E. Lowenstein publisher: Random House

"POOR CHARLIE'S ALMANACK: the Wisdom and Wit of Charlie Munger" publisher: Walsworth Publishing Co. Foreword by Warren Buffett

Then you must read:

All of Buffett's letter to his partners and shareholders, starting with the first that I know of in 1958 to the one he is going to write and release on February 26th 2022.

Plus, "The Super Investors of Graham and Doddsville" by Warren Buffett.
It is an incredible piece of work and causes me goosebumps every time I read it.

Then read every lecture, text, interview or anything you can find of Benjamin Graham's.

I never met a good investor that is not a voracious reader of many different types of inspiring, beneficial and enjoyable materials.
I just want you to focus for now on the key books, to make sure you don't make the mistake of reading a lot of books but forget to read and reread the essential ones.

I will add a list of books I would suggest you stay away from.

Especially those about asset allocations strategies and all that jazz; they really don't make any sense to me. But I don't want you to waste money on useless materials, money that could be wisely invested. Moreover, if you read the books I suggest, there's no fixed list you need. With Graham and Buffett as your guides, you will be able to recognize for yourself all the noise and funk from the "high priests" (in both books or financial courses) that are really just "twaddle".

The Joy of Investing
with **Marco Turco**

A sunrisewise publication

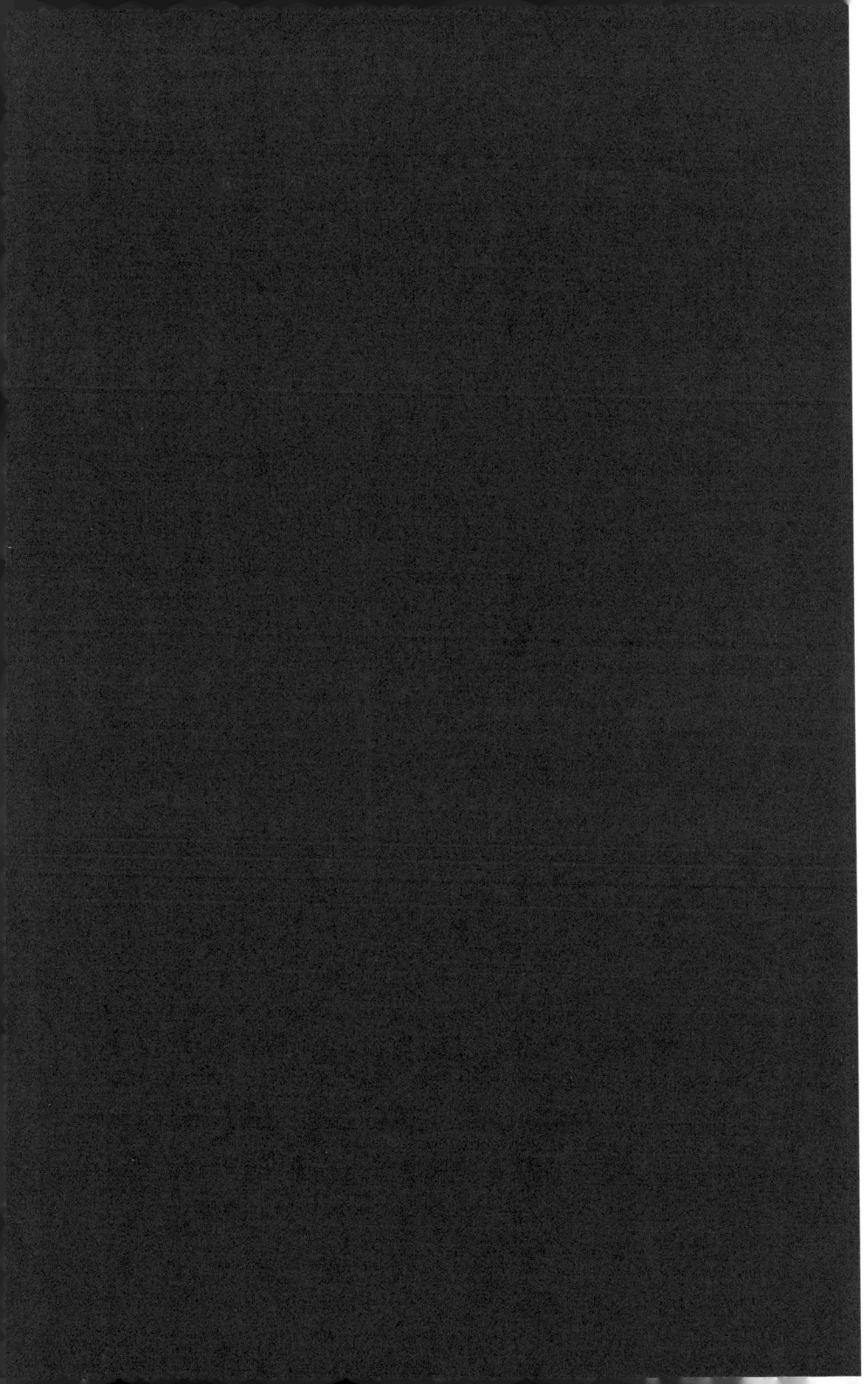